QUINCEAÑERA

THE ILAN STAVANS LIBRARY OF LATINO CIVILIZATION

QUINCEAÑERA

Edited by Ilan Stavans

GREENWOOD

AN IMPRINT OF ABC-CLIO, LLC
Santa Barbara, California • Denver, Colorado • Oxford, England

Library of Congress Cataloging-in-Publication Data

Quinceañera / edited by Ilan Stavans.
     p. cm.
  Includes bibliographical references and index.
  ISBN 978-0-313-35824-1 (hard copy : alk. paper)— ISBN 978-0-313-35825-8 (ebook)
  1. Quinceañera (Social custom)—United States. 2. Hispanic American teenage girls—Social life and customs. 3. Sex role—United States.
4. Hispanic Americans—Social life and customs. 5. Hispanic Americans—Rites and ceremonies. 6. Hispanic Americans—Ethnic identity. 7. United States—Ethnic relations. I. Stavans, Ilan.
  GT2490.Q85 2010
  305.235′208968073—dc22

2009047440

13 12 11 10 9   1 2 3 4 5

This book is also available on the World Wide Web as an eBook.
Visit www.abc-clio.com for details.

ABC-CLIO, LLC
130 Cremona Drive, P.O. Box 1911
Santa Barbara, California 93116-1911

This book is printed on acid-free paper ∞
Manufactured in the United States of America

Contents

SERIES FOREWORD

The book series *The Ilan Stavans Library of Latino Civilization*, the first of its kind, is devoted to exploring all the facets of Hispanic civilization in the United States, with its ramifications in the Americas, the Caribbean Basin, and the Iberian Peninsula. The objective is to showcase its richness and complexity from a myriad perspective. According to the U.S. Census Bureau, the Latino minority is the largest in the nation. It is also the fifth largest concentration of Hispanics in the globe.

One out of every seven Americans traces his or her roots to the Spanish-speaking world. Mexicans make up about 65% of the minority. Other major national groups are Puerto Ricans, Cubans, Dominicans, Ecuadorians, Guatemalans, Nicaraguans, Salvadorans, and Colombians. They are either immigrants, descendants of immigrants, or dwellers in a territory (Puerto Rico, the Southwest) having a conflicted relationship with the mainland U.S. As such, they are the perfect example of *encuentro*: an encounter with different social and political modes, an encounter with a new language, and encounter with a different way of dreaming.

The series is a response to the limited resources available and the abundance of stereotypes, which are a sign of lazy thinking. The 20th century Spanish philosopher José Ortega y Gasset, author of *The Revolt of the Masses*, once said: "By speaking, by thinking, we undertake to clarify things, and that forces us to exacerbate them, dislocate them, schematize them. Every concept is in itself an exaggeration." The purpose of the series is not to clarify but to complicate our understanding of Latinos. Do so many individuals from different national, geographic, economic, religious, and ethnic backgrounds coalesce as an integrated whole? Is there an *unum* in the *pluribus*?

Baruch Spinoza believed that every thing in the universe wants to be preserved in its present form: a tree wants to be a tree, and a dog a dog. Latinos in the United States want to be Latinos in the United States—no easy task, and therefore an intriguing one to explore. Each volume of the series contains an assortment of approximately a dozen articles, essays and interviews by journalists and specialists in their respective fields, followed by a bibliography of important resources on the topic. Their compilation is designed to generate debate and foster research: to complicate our knowledge. Every attempt is made to balance the ideological viewpoint of the authors. The target audience is students, specialists, and the lay reader. Themes will range from politics to sports, from music to cuisine. Historical periods and benchmarks like the Mexican War, the Spanish American War, the Zoot Suit Riots, the Bracero Program, and the Cuban Revolution, as well as controversial topics like Immigration, Bilingual Education, and Spanglish will be tackled.

Democracy is able to thrive only when it engages in an open, honest exchange of information. By offering diverse, insightful volumes about Hispanic life in the United States and inviting people to engage in critical thinking, *The Ilan Stavans Library of Latino Civilization* seeks to open new vistas to appreciate the fastest growing, increasingly heterogeneous minority in the nation—to be part of the *encuentro*.

Ilan Stavans

INTRODUCTION

Just like *Cinco de Mayo* and *Día de los Muertos*, over the years the *quinceañera* party, a tradition of the debutante ball, has acquired a distinct *gringo* taste. While it is celebrated in corners of the Spanish-speaking world, it has become an important social occasion in the Latino community in the United States, especially among Mexicans, Salvadorans, Dominicans, Puerto Ricans, and Cubans. It is a rite of passage whereby a girl, when turning fifteen years of age, is acknowledged as a full-fledged member of the community. The festivities include food, dance, and social interaction. They might last from a single day to a week and even a month. Not only does the immediate family invest money, time, and reputation, but the extended members also play an important part of the entourage. For instance, the *padrinos*—Spanish for godparents—might be asked to provide different components of the party, including the *quinceañera* dress.

The essays and *testimonios* in this collection approach the ceremonies from myriad perspectives. Karal Ann Marling, who teaches art at the University of Minnesota, places it in the context of "American Debdom" and the debutante's coming-of-age in various segments of American culture. Karen Mary Dávalos explores the connection between gender and ethnicity. The anthropologist Ruth Horowitz focuses on *quinceañera* in the Chicano community. Kristen Deiter meditates on the role of the Catholic Church as a spiritual benefactor, an important factor in recent times that stands in contrast with the fact that for years the Church didn't participate in the festivities. Indeed, not until 2007 and in response to the growing popularity of the tradition did the United States Conference on Catholic Bishops issue a formal ritual for the occasion, never having had one before. Valentina Napolitano researched the *quinceañera* in Guadalajara, Mexico. She makes an argument for conceiving the ritual as directly linked to images of femaleness, family status, and respectability in Mexican society. And Sara Arcaya, along with Bianca Salazar and other students at Somerville Charter High School, in Boston, Massachusetts, follows similar lines, studying *in situ* the connection between race, class, culture, and religion. For each of these authors, the concept of performance is fundamental to the understanding of the celebration.

The volume concludes with snapshot pieces by writer Judith Ortiz-Cofer, who reminisces about turning fifteen in her native Puerto Rico, and Julia Alvarez, the Dominican author of *How the García Girls Lost Their Accent*, who spent a year researching the *quinceañera* phenomenon in the United States. Finally, Francisca "Panchita" Dávila, a dressmaker in a small town in upstate New York, talks about her personal experience as a community seamstress.

PART I
PREPARATIVOS

Quinceañera Debutante: Rites and Regalia of American Debdom

Karal Ann Marling

The origins of the quinceañera (quince for short)—a gala celebration of a girl's fifteenth birthday—are obscure. Some say that it is an ancient Aztec initiation rite taken over by the Catholic Church in the sixteenth century. Or a ceremony begun in the nineteenth century by Carlota, the Austrian Empress of Mexico and the Duchess of Alba, on the model of European court debuts. Many American clergy pressured into opening a daylong and highly secular quinceañera with a religious service maintain that it is no more than an invented tradition, liable to bankrupt the family of the girl so honored; to them, it is a wanton display of material wealth and procreative potential that ought not be sanctioned by the church.

However, anthropologists doing fieldwork in remote villages in the Andes have encountered similar ceremonies for both girls and boys, signaling their readiness for marriage. In preparation for the party, the teenagers are expected to act like adults by performing good works in the community and in the church. Tourists and vacationers have come upon "Mis Quince Años" observances, complete with white dress and tiara, all over rural Latin America and Cuba. Until the 1960s, however, the quinceañera was rare among Latin populations eager to assimilate quietly into suburban America. Or the ritual was absorbed into look-alike debuts: in Chicago, the Cordi-Marian Cotillion; in El Paso, the Symphony Debut; in Zapata County, Texas, the Quinceañera Ball.

In its most highly developed recent form, the American quinceañera leaves conventional debuts in the shade. Except for Cubans and Puerto Ricans, who have discarded most of the religious portions of the ceremony, the day begins with a Mass or a blessing at which the young woman renews her baptismal vows and commits herself to a virtuous adult life. Often she comes to church dressed as a bride, in a long white gown. The bell-shaped skirts favored for the occasion are thought to reflect Spanish court dress of the imperial past. Accompanying the *quinceañera* to church are relatives, who present her with a

Karal Ann Marling: "*Quinceañera* Debutante," included in *Debutante: Rites and Regalia in American Debdom*. Lawrence: University of Kansas Press, 2004.

religious medal and a Bible or prayer book, and members of her official reti-
nue: a *chambelán* (also known as the *galán* or the *escorte*), who can be a father, a
brother, or an out-and-out date; a court of honor composed of fourteen young
couples, who stand for the years of her life (a half-court will do just as well
to maintain the symbolism); and godparents, along with other *padrinos* and
madrinas who have made material contributions to the festivities. If a church
service is held, it is often climaxed by a dressing ritual in which the girl's
mother puts a tiara or crown on her head while her father removes her flats
and replaces them with the high-heeled shoes of womanhood.

These semi-sacramental components of the quinceañera can also be folded
into a reception or party organized along the lines of a debut grafted onto a
Broadway musical, a senior prom, and a dream wedding. In addition to the
redressing of the *quinceañera*, the *chambelán* or a hired MC introduces the other
members of the court and the young lady of the hour, who curtsies to the guests
and opens a series of dances: rehearsed numbers performed by the court and
the kinds of girl-and-father, mother-and-date ballroom dancing—the *vals*, or
waltz—associated with wedding receptions. This activity takes place in a lav-
ishly decorated room often featuring stage sets made or rented for the evening: arbors, Cinderella coaches, giant seashells, or a wicker peacock throne
enhanced with lace, ribbons, and artificial flowers, where she sits for the shoe
exchange. There are toasts, thank-yous to the sponsors, and a response from
the *quinceañera* in which she expresses gratitude for her upbringing. A dinner and a less formal dance follow, with a DJ, and everyone joining in. There
are printed programs listing the sponsors and their offerings. A multi-tiered
cake embellished with statuary and fountains. Favors for the guests in the
form of *capias* (ribbons) or *cerámicas* (figurines). A satin-covered photo album.
A ceremonial pillow on which the birthday girl may kneel at church; if the
service is omitted, the pillow can be used to present each of the traditional
gifts—earrings, a bracelet, a medal or necklace, the crown, a bouquet, and so
forth. Elaboration of the symbolic gifts speaks to a growing prosperity among
those of Latin heritage. The objects themselves, available from professional,
paid planners, may have originated in the markets of Guadalajara, from which
many of the costly, brand-new "traditional" aspects of the rite are said to come.

The gaudiest, six-figure quinceañeras are held among the Cuban exiles of
Miami. Girls have been known to drop into swimming pools from helicop-
ters at the moment of introduction. Dance numbers performed by the *damas*
and their partners are choreographed by experts and perfected for months
on end. Nothing is too good, too big, too expensive for the fifteen-year-old
daughter of the house. The age at which the ritual is enacted may be the most
traditional thing about a modern-day quince, although even here, Mexican-
American families have begun to hold "Sweet Sixteen" parties using the same
props and iconography. So this is clearly meant to be a teenage rite of passage,
something like the old-style debut tea that marked the completion of a girl's
domestic education. But throughout the later twentieth century, the age of the
average debutante crept upward to accommodate college plans: maturity, in
Anglo society, was deferred longer and longer, until the debut itself became
laughably redundant. After her presentation, the *quinceañera* can act like a

woman. She can date, wear makeup, take responsibility for many of her own decisions. In the social climate of today's America, to be sure, she has already done most of these grown-up things before the magic age of fifteen. But the choice of fifteen as the symbolic moment of transition masks parental fears that their teenager may lose her virtue as well as her home-taught values in the permissive ambience of a Phoenix or a Fort Worth high school. An unsuccessful movement to develop a quince for boys was organized in the 1970s to prevent them from joining criminal gangs.

In the preference for a teen debut, Latinos—like African Americans—acknowledge the threat posed to the young by mass culture and the loosening of family bonds. But unlike black debuts, in which the emphasis falls squarely on education and betterment, the quinceañera aims to legitimate and control the sexuality of the pubescent girl. She is ready to be a wife, a sexual being, says the bridal regalia. She is grown-up and a member of a successful clan that is able to shower her with jewelry, finery, limos, and all manner of pretty, feminine souvenirs of her big day. She is Cinderella, off to the ball. No wedding could be quite as wonderful: then, she will have to share the spotlight with the groom! The arguments of a fretful clergy opposed to the ruinous extravagance of the quinceañera, the celebration of biological maturity, and the overt sexual promise of many facets of the ceremony are probably valid. So is their belief that this is a synthetic, inauthentic ritual. But none of these objections cuts to the heart of debbing or quincing: honoring oneself and one's female offspring and giving mothers, who are in charge of such happenings, the chance to validate their lives, their maternity, and the power that the bloom of youth uniquely accords to girls at this time of life.

The case for an intense level of maternal involvement is similar to defenses of beauty pageants for children in the wake of the Jon Benét Ramsey murder case. Indeed, many of the same mall shops and Internet retailers that supply quinceañera finery for fifteen-year-olds also purvey all the accessories needed to transform a five-year-old into a miniature version of Miss America. And it cannot be coincidental that the venues in which the quinceañera thrives—the border states and the warm-weather South—are also prime spawning grounds for big-time pageant culture. Many of the "inauthentic" aspects of the quince come straight from the world of the beauty contest: a staged show, "theme" parties with semi-professional dance routines, tiaras ("Just like Princess Diana's!" reads one ad; "Just like Audrey Hepburn!"), high heels, big hair, and a sparkly white dress.

Every one of the competitors in the 2001 Miss America Pageant, televised live from Atlantic City, wore a white, fairy-tale gown for the opening introductions. For the "evening-wear" competition, the twenty semifinalists, most still in white, were led to the stage by a father or a brother to make a formal bow to the audience. If the beauty pageant is a democratic, mass-media coming out, then the Miss America contest, since 1921, has been crowning the nation's designated Deb of the Year—or our prettiest, peppiest *quiceañera*. Even in swimsuits, most pageant contestants still wear their ceremonial high heels.

Although the Misses America can be counted on to entertain troops and avoid seditious comments to the press, they are not primarily involved with perpetuating or honoring the American heritage. But the quinceañera, whatever its importations from movie and pageant land, is about having Latino or Hispanic ancestry. Even the most assimilated high school sophomore, in this one rite of passage, acknowledges her ethnicity. Ethnic pride is another legacy of the civil rights movement of the 1960s: the quince, and other hyphenated celebrations, grew in popularity as it became socially viable to admit to "different" geographic origins, menus, customs, and ideals. Insofar as those ideals include premarital chastity and eventual motherhood for girls, the quinceañera accurately portrays old-country expectations, even as they come under increasing pressure from contemporary culture at large. Quincing is about retaining respect for the old ways, even if they are sometimes honored in startling new forms.

One of the ironies of life in Texas, on the permeable Mexican border, is the turnabout appropriation of Latino culture by well-to-do Anglos. The civic debut rituals of San Antonio are a good example of make-believe Mexicanism, which is also an essential part of California festival life, including the Santa Barbara Fiesta and the Tournament of Roses Parade in Pasadena. In San Antonio, a Battle of the Flowers Parade inaugurated in 1891 spawned the Fiesta, which, like the Veiled Prophet celebrations in St. Louis, eventually became the exclusive purview of white debs of good family. The distinctive mark of the Fiesta queen (and her numerous attendants) is a custom-made court robe that trails to fantastic lengths and is decorated in giant embroidered patterns enriched with glass jewels and/or tiny mirrors, all the better to glitter under artificial light. The gowns are so heavy and stiff that debs often need to be transported to their runway in an open-bed pickup. In addition, San Antonio Coronation debutantes disappoint the crowd unless—robe and all—they perform that infamous "Texas dip" in which the lady's forehead actually grazes the floor, in imitation of Pavlova's pose at the end of the second act of *Swan Lake*.

Columnist Molly Ivins, sharp-tongued chronicler of all things Texan, observed that the overwhelming too-muchness of the San Antonio Fiesta has cast its spell over all types of comings out in that state. "Texas debutantes are like Las Vegas or a thousand-pound cheese or a submarine sandwich as long as a football field," she wrote in 1991. "Doesn't matter whether you like it or not—you have to admit that it's really something. Even if you can't define what." So Texas families, going Detroit tycoons of an earlier day one better, see nothing amiss in hiring civic auditoriums and complete circuses to entertain at their daughters' coming-out parties. Likewise, at a good, new-fashioned Texas quinceañera, no quantity of baubles and furbelows and fripperies is too excessive for the moment when the little *niña* becomes a full-blown bride-to-be. Whether the debutante is black, white, brown, rich, working class, a college girl, or a bright-eyed high school kid bent on a career in local politics, her moment in the limelight ought to be "really something." Fluffy. Glitzy. Buoyant. Odd. An event to remember, even if you can't quite grasp what happened.

La Quinceañera: Making Gender and Ethnic Identities

Karen Mary Dávalos

The church looked empty, but I could hear a man talking to someone about how late it was getting. He complained that the girl and her family had not yet arrived, and he was scheduled to perform a wedding in less than an hour. He sounded angry, so I glanced only briefly at the plastic and natural flowers decorating the pews and the statue of the *Virgen de Guadalupe* before heading inside. Those guests who had arrived stood on the church steps and showed no interest in entering the Byzantine building.

The guests, some dressed in blue jeans and others in formal clothes, greeted each other and talked about the girl of honor. They didn't stand, washed and quiet, in circles and whisper amongst themselves. No, there was a feeling of familiarity and confidence as the guests mingled around greeting and kissing each other on the cheek. This was not an idle or impatient wait, but a moment for friends and family to catch up on family news, especially news about the girl of honor. However, even when the greetings slowed down to a trickle, no one made a move to go inside. People remained waiting on the steps.

After several minutes, the family began to arrive in small groups. The mother of the girl, bringing a bouquet of flowers, looked tired but happy. Next, the eldest sister arrived with her husband. The girl's brothers brought more flowers and gifts. One brother ran from his car to find the pastor. He called out to me, saying that his sister's limousine had not shown up at the house. Finally, the girl whose fifteenth year we were celebrating and her oldest brother drove up in a dark blue Lincoln Continental. This was the moment for which we had been waiting.

Karen Mary Dávalos: "*La Quinceañera*: Making Gender and Ethnic Identities," first published in *Frontiers: A Journal of Women Studies*, vol. 16, nos. 2–3, Gender, Nations, and Nationalisms (1996): 101–27. Reprinted in *Perspectives on Las Américas: A Reader in Culture, History, and Representation*, edited by Matthew C. Gutmann, Félix V. Matos Rodríguez, Lynn Stephan, and Patricia Zavalla. Malden: Blackwell Publishers, 2003.

MAKING GENDER AND ETHNIC IDENTITIES THROUGH
CULTURAL PRACTICES

The above story, which comes from my fieldnotes made during dissertation research in Chicago (1990–1992) among *mexicanas* and their families, deliberately leaves the reader at the door of the church waiting for the special
celebration to begin.[1] Although the special celebration, called *la quinceañera*,
is the concern of this paper, I avoid writing my own representation of this
public and familial event because I want to examine how others describe and
experience *la quinceañera*.[2] The strategy to highlight the *mexicana* voices of my
"field notes" is influenced by fieldwork experiences, university training, and
indirect schooling from Chicano ethnographers.

As a self-identified *mexicana* (when in the Midwest) and Chicana (when in
the Southwest), I have often been told that my dissertation research was auto-
ethnographic or that I am an "insider." In my years as a student, I felt that
this rhetorical comment was an attack or a defense. However, from fieldwork
I have found that the everyday dance of getting to know someone, finding
one's way through a city, and making mistakes demonstrates how anthropology mystifies the landscape by imposing a cartography of "outsiders" and
"insiders" onto a world that is described as "cultural."[3] Patricia Zavella's fieldwork experiences and candid reflection on them encourage us to reexamine
the cartography. Zavella, a self-identified Chicana feminist, eloquently writes
of her experience as an "insider" conducting fieldwork among women can-
nery workers in the Santa Clara Valley of California and how she makes the
mistake of assuming her identity will "provide ready access to this community of informants." She tells how her "privileges as an educated woman" and
her feminism made her an "outsider," creating "some awkward moments."[4]

Not only did I experience awkward moments, *mexicanas* explicitly made
me an insider or outsider. *Mexicanas* told me at various times that I was "too
dark," that my Spanish was "too perfect," or that "I should have known better." They reversed the color line with which I was familiar (brown skin as the
sign of the authentic Chicano), they exploded the rule I had learned in college
(fluency in the "native" language promotes rapport with one's informants),
and they scolded me for not being what I appeared to be (someone like themselves). Comments such as these blurred the boundaries between "insider"
and "outsider" and forced me to realize that I could never speak for these
mexicanas, only find partial representations of them in my "field notes."

From university-based experiences, I was inspired by the work of James
Clifford and Renato Rosaldo, who encourage readers to examine how ethnog-
raphies are made and how ethnographers authenticate their work.[5] Clifford
writes convincingly about writing styles and strategies used by ethnographers
to project a false image of an objective, detached social scientist. Rosaldo ad-
vises his contemporaries to imagine themselves as "positioned subjects" who
"grasp certain human phenomena better than others" over their lifetime.[6] He
tells how his own experience with death made him better able to examine
Ilongot emotions. In fact, Rosaldo reminds us, ethnographers usually begin
rethinking and revising their project (or perspective) while in the field.[7] The
changing perspectives that I anticipated, along with an awareness about writ-

ing for academic authority, led me to recognize that this ethnography cannot pretend to be a "unified master summation" about the *quinceañera* and the *mexicanas* who engage in one.[8]

University-based experiences also encouraged me to examine how writing strategies echo larger theoretical perspectives and agendas. The work of third world feminists, such as Chandra T. Mohanty and Gloria Anzaldúa, argues that western feminists who imagine that they are "speaking for" third world women rely on the perspective that dominated women cannot speak for themselves.[9] They each suggest that the process of decolonizing feminist anthropology requires that we study women as active agents, not just exploited and oppressed victims. Therefore, I avoid a general description of the *quinceañera* because I have a third world feminist concern with how *mexicanas*, as social analysts, construct the event and "have a critical perspective on their own situation."[10] I argue that what *mexicanas* have to say about the *quinceañera* can tell us how they construct themselves as historical and oppositional subjects. In addition to paying attention to human agency, I follow Anzaldúa's argument that in the context of domination *mexicanas* invent new meanings and knowledges for their lives that are both creative and contradictory. That is, their agency is not a heroic response to oppression but a negotiation between various, often conflicting, views about women, family, and *mexicano* culture.

My focus on the negotiation and contestation surrounding the event encourages a rethinking of "tradition." The arguments over the *quinceañera* do not spring from misinformation or miscommunication but are indicative of the thing itself. Instead of searching for the "real" or "traditional" *quinceañera*, I seek to discuss "tradition" as an open, and sometimes chaotic, terrain that is constantly reconfigured in everyday experience. The text tries to reflect this fluidity by not taking too seriously (or reifying) the descriptions and categories that invoke the "traditional." For example, during the period of my field research (May 25, 1990 to November 8, 1992), Catholic clergy and laity entered into a heated argument about the most "traditional" meanings and practices that constitute the *quinceañera*. I do not try to settle the argument, but interpret the debate as the ongoing construction of "tradition" by the people who are attributed with traditionality.

Indirect, though consistent, training by Chicano ethnographers also influenced my writing and field strategy. This training was not a formal part of my university instruction but resulted from happenstance encounters in the hallway or classroom with Chicano professors who would recommend a book or an article. Like many students of Chicano culture, I read Octavio Romano and Américo Paredes who taught me to distrust anthropological accounts of Mexican Americans that rely on a cultural determinism model.[11] After the smoke cleared and the cultural determinism model was found dead, a more lasting lesson encouraged us to attack anthropology's tendency to abuse its informants by not offering an exchange for information and intrusion. Because of this legacy of abuse, many Chicano ethnographers are determined to "give something back" to the community in which they study. Maxine Baca Zinn identifies non-exploitative reciprocity and exchange as a particular concern of Chicano ethnographers doing research among Chicanos.[12] My approach in the field was to offer my friendship; assistance with employment and employment training; educational counsel; the use of my computer, printer, and typewriter (especially to make résumés); and photographic services at family events (including *quinceañera*) in exchange for a place in people's lives. Post-fieldwork commitments include continued friendship, educational counsel, translation, and writing. *Mexicanas* encouraged me to expand the notion of "giving something back" to include the documentation of their experiences. They repeatedly told me and each other that they were eager to read "my book" about their lives. During my first return to Chicago (July 2 through August 10, 1994), we spent most of our time together reading my dissertation. For them, the dissertation (and subsequent writing) is a kind of reclaiming of cultural memory, a witness to their past and for their future.[13]

POINT OF REFERENCE

In what follows, I examine the ways in which people regard the *quinceañera*. For ease of illustration, my analysis is divided into two parts. When read together, the two parts of this paper bring to light how particular explanations, descriptions, and forms of the *quinceañera* are embedded within people's ideas about appropriate gender roles, ethnic identity, traditional culture, sexuality, class position, and anticipated results of culture contact. The first part examines how Catholic priests and journalists regard the event. The popular discussion by Catholic officials and the media enjoys wider circulation and authority than the discussions I heard among *mexicanas* and their families, taken up in the second part of the paper. However, these two parts should not be made to stand for distinct or homogeneous communities that are inherently opposed to each other.

Let me briefly explain. First, there was considerable disagreement among Catholic worshippers, particularly *mexicanas* and their daughters, over the form of the *quinceañera*. They argued over the format, aesthetics, and design of the event. Second, complicated life experiences of members of this group make it difficult to describe them as "immigrants" or to categorize them by "generation." Although the more than forty *mexicanas* that I met in Chicago all have legal standing in the United States and have been raised in Chicago, they have various ties to Mexico and the United States as a homeplace. Half of the women consistently travel to Mexico, spending their summer or winter vacations there. Between the ages of fifteen and twenty-one, *mexicanas* might spend up to six months in Mexico. *Mexicanas* with children told me that they deliberately traveled to Mexico during a child's first few years so that the infant could learn to speak Spanish. Family members from Mexico also "vacation" in Chicago. The length of the visit often depends on the job market, upcoming family celebrations, and emotional ties. At any given time, I could visit households composed of both Mexican and United States citizens, the former often becoming a significant part of my research. In addition, I found several households in which United States citizenship did not indicate someone's place of birth or their homeplace. In one family the first and third child were born in Mexico, while the second and last in the United States. The parents, one born in the United States and the other a naturalized U.S. citizen, had "returned" to Mexico after retirement. Dispersion, travel, and reterritorialization better describe their experiences.

In the same light, we must recognize that Catholic officials do not come from discrete communities. Many of Chicago's Spanish-speaking clergy are from Spain and Poland. The Chicago Archdiocese requires that those who minister to *mexicano* neighborhoods such as Pilsen, Little Village, Back of the Yards, and South Chicago have a functional understanding of Spanish. Language ability, however, reveals nothing about one's multicultural sensibilities, so that even the *mexicano* parishes with origins in the 1920s find little support from the Archdiocese of Chicago.[14] Multicultural insensitivity is the result of a history of Americanization efforts within the Archdiocese of Chicago and a legacy of national parishes that promoted xenophobia rather than interethnic tolerance. Nonetheless, the Hispanic Caucus, composed of clergy who minister to Spanish-speaking neighborhoods, attempts to hold the Archdiocese accountable to the needs of *mexicano* and Puerto Rican worshippers. The Hispanic Caucus does not, however, have a united perspective on the *quinceañera*.

Although I am not willing to generalize about the *quinceañera* in an attempt to encourage readers to focus on different voices and discourses, other ethnographers and journalists have been willing to do so. I include their accounts of the *quinceañera* to provide the reader with a point of reference. The following accounts compare a *quinceañera* to a bar mitzvah, to a Southern debutante coming-out party, and to a wedding.

In one of two Chicago ethnographic accounts,[15] anthropologist Gwen Stern had this to say about a "traditional" *quinceañera*:

> [It] can be an elaborate event, equal to a wedding, in both time and expense.[16]
>
> The first part of the quinceañera involves a mass in church where the girl gives thanks for guidance and makes a promise before the altar of the Virgin of Guadalupe. There is a procession up the aisle, with the girl on her father's arm, preceded by her attendants. During the mass, the religious medal is presented to the girl by her padrinos, and blessed by the priest.[17]
>
> Less affluent families, and less traditional ones, may simply give a birthday party on a daughter's fifteenth birthday, since a full-fledged quinceañera is an expensive affair.[18]

Although Stern's dissertation rejects the acculturation and assimilation models popular in the 1960s and early 1970s, her account of the *quinceañera* assumes that the contents of people's lives can be reduced to "more or less" traditional. Stern produces a code for behavior instead of her goal to take a "process-oriented approach" sensitive to how actors "manipulate symbols."[19]

Journalist David Beard also focused on the movement of the girl and her attendants, making it easy to compare the event to a wedding. His lengthy article for *Lifestyle*, a Sunday supplement in the *Chicago Tribune*, was accompanied by photographs of the girl dancing, her father and mother, and the reception.

A court of 14 couples slowly strolled down the center aisle as the organist played the processional. At the altar each couple parted, the girls turning left and the boys turning right. Only the girl in white satin remained; her head tilted downward in a show of respectful deference; heavy breaths moved her shoulders up and down, betraying feelings of expectation and fear. Her father walked to her left; her mother to her right.

There was only one person missing—the groom. In a *quinceañera* (keen-sa-an-YAIR-uh), a Mexican celebration of a girl's 15th birthday that dates back to the Aztecs, there is no groom. It is hard for non-Mexicans to understand the fiesta *quinceañera* (Spanish for "15th party"), although hundreds are performed each year in Chicago, especially in later summer and early autumn. Think of it as a social debut. Or as a Catholic bar mitzvah for girls.[20]

Ten years later, Constanza Montaña, the *Chicago Tribune*'s specialist on Latino events, also described the procession.

Fourteen young women in long pink gowns, escorted by 14 young men wearing high school ROTC uniforms, walked down the aisle at St. Philomena's Catholic Church in the North Side neighborhood of Hermosa recently. They were followed by a little boy in tails and a little girl in a formal dress, each carrying a white satin pillow.

As they filed into the pews, the young people turned to watch the slow steps of Candy Marroquin as she approached the altar.

The flower-decked church had all the trappings of a wedding. But the guests were not there to witness Candy's marriage vows. Rather, they had come to celebrate her 15th birthday, a tradition known in Latin America as *quinceañera*.[21]

Let me remind the reader that these brief accounts should not serve as general descriptions, codes for behavior, or predictions. By themselves they tell little about the quality and politics of the event, and perhaps they reveal more about the writers than about the practice itself. The descriptive narrative and the focus on material features of the event places the accounts in the genres of journalism and classic ethnography. (Both genres proclaim to report "the truth.") Constanza Montaña even borrows the now-classic trope from ethnography and uses shock and surprise to allow readers to imagine Candy Marroquin and her family as exotic foreigners whose confusing behavior requires translation. Nevertheless, the accounts provide a point of reference for the reader.

EXPLAINING THE *QUINCEAÑERA*

Catholic officials, journalists, and social scientists in Chicago have shown striking similarity in their description of the *quinceañera*. Between 1971 and 1991 there are repeatedly uniform descriptions and explanations of the event in daily newspapers, dissertations, research reports, parish bulletins, diocesan guidelines for a *quinceañera* service, and internal Catholic periodicals written by and for church officials.[22] I refer to these manuscripts as the public discourse on the *quinceañera*. Although not the Archdiocese's spokesperson for popular religiosity or the Spanish-speaking ministry, Rev. Peter Rodriguez is the most prolific and most cited author on the *quinceañera*. Perhaps due to his exposure from serving at Chicago's historically important Mexican parishes (the Northside's St. Francis of Assisi and the Southside's Immaculate Heart of Mary), Rev. Rodriguez has gained a reputation as the local authority on the event. The other Catholic officials participating in the public discourse are members of the Hispanic Caucus, including Rev. Arturo Pérez, pastor of former St. Casmir, Rev. Charles Dahm, pastor of St. Pius V, and Rev. Juan Huitrado, pastor of former St. Vitus Parish.[23] Each ministers in predominantly *mexicano* neighborhoods.

Within the public discourse, the *quinceañera* is regarded in three ways: as an extension of particular Catholic sacraments, as a rite of passage, and as a practice that has historical continuity or "tradition." Similar descriptions, however, are not based on similar projects. Some journalists and clergy write about the *quinceañera* to convince other Catholic officials of its significance. They imply that priests who refuse to celebrate the *quinceañera* are not acting in a Christian way. More critically, a few priests refer to papal decrees that promote popular religiosity and cultural diversity within the Catholic Church. Writing for a clerical audience, Rev. Arturo Bañuelas reminds clergy of their duty to "support the religious expressions of the common people."[24] Rev. William Conway, in a series of articles on the importance of the *quinceañera*, refers to a papal sermon in which clergy are encouraged to "respect the integrity of the culture in which they are working."[25] Turning to necessity and not papal authority, Rev. Pérez argues that the *quinceañera* is an "opportunity for evangelization," or a "teachable moment," that clergy should not refuse.[26] The opportunity to evangelize, he claims, is important because most youth do not attend church services.

Other clergy and journalists attempt to convince the reader that worshippers who celebrate the *quinceañera* are misguided. This literature reflects a national trend to regulate popular forms of religiosity among *mexicano* worshippers.[27] Clergy argue that worshippers can be misguided in two ways: first, they are overly concerned with money and social prestige, and second, with sex. *Mexicano* worshippers, Catholic officials claim, have made the event into a farce because they spend too much money or because they encourage sexual activity among youth. In 1990, Rev. David Pavlic, the pastor of Providence of God parish in the predominantly *mexicano* neighborhood of Pilsen, argued that "the families that throw these often go into tremendous debt . . . [and] I have a problem with the message of the ceremony: 'Here's the girl and she's ripe for the picking.'"[28] Rev. Pavlic was adamant that not only is it against Catholic principles to encourage sexual activity among unmarried youth, but it is unethical "when you have a situation, not just among Hispanics but among all youth today, where you see so much teen pregnancy."[29]

Journalists Lisa Holton, Constanza Montaña, and Jorge Casuso each report what Casuso identifies as a "rift between the church hierarchy and the many in the Hispanic [Mexican] community" over the cost of the event.[30] However,

Holton's article did not appear in the municipal or religious section but in the business section. In this cover page article complete with a table detailing the "Hispanic Market," Holton describes how "Hispanic consumers" spend thousands of dollars on a *quinceañera*. She quotes owners and managers of bridal shops and department stores who attest to the rapidly growing business in dresses for the *quinceañera*. Holton claims that despite the various forms for a *quinceañera*, retailers can count on one mainstay—the dress—which she reassures them costs from $100 to $500. Ed Kubicki, manager of a department store, calculates for the reader that this can add up since "there may be as many as 14 attendants" in the celebration.[31]

Despite their differing justifications for the event, Catholic priests and journalists describe the "most genuine" *quinceañera* in similar ways. The following attributes are repeatedly found in the public discourse on the *quinceañera*. The ceremony begins with a procession to the church in which the parents accompany their daughter. During the ceremony the girl prays to God in order to renew her baptismal commitment, to strengthen her faith, to ask for a blessing as she enters a new stage in life, to give thanks for arriving at the age of fifteen, and to honor her parents. The ceremony focuses on the relationships between the parents and their daughter and between God and the family. Local guidelines recommend that the *quinceañera* "should be celebrated in the spirit of prayer, solemnity, simplicity and festivity."[32]

Many clergy are explicit about the number of attendants, the kinds of objects allowed in the ceremony, and who may sponsor the girl. Increasingly, family sponsors [*padrinos*/godparents] are limited to baptismal godparents or members of the nuclear family. In the late 1970s, Rev. Peter Rodriguez, while at Immaculate Heart of Mary in the Back of the Yards, argued that the use of *padrinos*, attendants, an escort for the girl, rings, medals, pillows, and a bouquet of flowers are "totally strange to the festivity" and were "impurities recently adopted in cities such as Guadalajara."[33] According to Rev. Rodriguez, objects are attributed with authenticity if they can be "traced" to Mexico or if they do not resemble the objects used in Catholic weddings. He implied that the *quinceañera* should not resemble a wedding precisely because of what a wedding ceremony permits: sexual activity and expression.

As early as 1971 Rodriguez had begun to restrict the participation of young men in an effort to limit heterosexual expression. The *chambelan*[34] who escorted the girl was naturalized as the catalyst for heterosexual encounters. In that year, church officials and lay leaders of St. Francis of Assisi, under the guidance of Peter Rodriguez, issued the following statement:

> The *quinceañera* is profoundly a religious and Christian celebration ... [I]t is contradictory and with negative effects that the *quinceañera* [the girl] arrive at the church accompanied by chamberlains: in little pairs as if they are engaged to each other. *In our Parish, we will not admit quinceañeras accompanied by young men.* Young men should be invited to the celebration of the Mass and the fiesta, but they are NOT allowed in the procession entering the church.[35]

Ignoring other types of sexual activity (such as father–daughter incest), by 1980 several parishes in the Chicago Archdiocese codified the practice of having both parents or the father escort the daughter into and out of the church. When I arrived in Chicago a decade later, Catholic officials referred to the parental escort as a traditional practice.

QUINCEAÑERA AS RITE OF PASSAGE

Invariably, Catholic officials and journalists describe and legitimate the *quinceañera* as a traditional religious ceremony that marks a rite of passage into adulthood. Several clergy and journalists specifically define adulthood as a movement from an irresponsible to a responsible member of society and church.[36] Adulthood, however, is not a generic stage of the life cycle, but one that is embedded in Catholic expectations of a woman.

According to Rev. Bañuelas, the ancient "initiation rite" on which the *quinceañera* is based taught girls "to be virtuous and to care for the poor and the handicapped."[37] His claim to "tradition" legitimated his argument that a contemporary "young woman could work on a project with the poor. She could participate in several community programs: visits to the elderly, [serve] meals on wheels, or help the handicapped."[38] During an interview, Rev. Arturo Perez claimed that "adulthood" was a time when "you start saying, 'I give' ... and not thinking of yourself." Childhood, he explained, was a time when girls are allowed to "think only about themselves," but adulthood is a time that they should "think of others first." His ideas echo a statement made in 1980 by Rev. Peter Rodriguez. At that time, Rev. Rodriguez argued that at the age of fifteen "the girl is not a child anymore. She cannot blame her parents for her faults. She is now entering the responsibility of womanhood."[39] In one of his most explicit instructions for womanhood, Rodriguez argued that after the event, "The responsibility lies with the girl to preserve her [sexual] purity until her wedding day."[40]

However, as Rodriguez admits, the church cannot trust that girls will understand or accept this responsibility without proper instruction.[41] Therefore, several clergy require that girls attend special classes prior to the event. In 1980 Rodriguez required that girls in his parish "give a confession and discuss personal values."[42] In a manuscript he shared with me, Rev. Pérez outlined a three-month program in which young girls develop specific plans to help their family, their friends, and their parish.[43] At St. Casmir, Pérez initiated a mandatory weekend program for all youth who wished to participate in the procession and the ceremony. After a year of refusing to celebrate the event at St. Pius V, Rev. Dahm decided that mandatory classes for the girl, her family, and her *padrinos* taught over four weekends would allow him to instruct the entire family about Catholic views on womanhood, service, and the family. At St. Vitus, Rev. Huitrado required the girl and her escorts to meet four times to reflect on the family, hope, and dignity. Interviews revealed that Pérez, Dahm, and Huitrado were ultimately concerned with the girl's virginity, but they employed code words such as "family" and "dignity" to disguise this focus.

According to Catholic officials and journalists, the *quinceañera* is an extension of baptism, an opportunity for conversion, and a chance to encourage young girls to begin a life of service. Church officials emphasize the role the *quinceañera* plays in bringing people to the church and in teaching gender roles and cultural traditions. Through the *quinceañera*, Catholic priests provide instruction to parents on how to educate their daughters about gender roles, "female" behavior, and sexuality. The regulation on family sponsors codifies the nuclear family as the legitimate participants in a *quinceañera* and as legitimate participants in the structuring of a girl's sexual and ethnic identity. *Mexicanas* and their families who refuse to follow Church requirements or who practice the *quinceañera* in ways not approved by their pastor are referred to as untraditional, pagan, amoral, unfit parents, or "lacking [cultural] identity."[44]

QUINCEAÑERA AS CONTINUITY: HISTORY AND TRADITION

Catholic officials, social scientists, and journalists claim that the *quinceañera* is a tradition or custom that has historical origins or roots. People who regard the *quinceañera* as historical or traditional are usually attempting to convince other clergy to celebrate the event. That is, they view the *quinceañera* as a legitimate "tradition" from Mexico and part of a legitimate popular faith. Catholic officials who want to defend the *quinceañera* as a form of popular religiosity do so by using history.

Most claim that the *quinceañera* has roots in or comes from indigenous cultures of Latin America, but different times and places are credited. In the last twenty years, the *quinceañera* is said to have "come from Mexico,"[45] from an "ancient European social custom" that was later "adopted in Latin America,"[46] and from the "Aztec Empire in Mexico."[47] By 1990, journalists and church officials narrowed their claims to Aztec and Mayan cultures. The following are some accounts of the origins of the *quinceañera*.

In 1975 Rev. Peter Rodriguez claimed that the *quinceañera* has European origins. In his Spanish-language weekly column in the archdiocesan newspaper, Rev. Rodriguez suggested that the contemporary practice can be attributed to Latin Americans who "changed the meaning" of the event.

> The *quinceañera* celebration has its origins in an ancient European social custom that had been the last part of a public presentation of young girls when they arrived at the age of taking part in society. In Europe the age for this ceremony was eighteen years old, or that age at which a woman becomes an adult according to civil and religious law. When this ceremony was adopted in the Latin American countries, the age of the ceremony was reduced to fifteen. . . . They added new elements that at the time enriched the ceremony and they significantly changed the meaning.[48]

Five years later, the agents of historical change were different. In 1980 journalist David Beard imagined that Spaniards transformed the event, not the people of the New World:

It began in the 15th Century with the rise of the Aztec Empire in Mexico. With a life expectancy rate of 30 years, the *quinceañera* marked the midway point of an Aztec girl's life, the time when she would become a woman and marry. She was officially presented to the tribe, an event that kept the fathers of pretty young girls busy sorting and selecting marriage offers. When the Spaniards arrived in the 16th Century, traces of Catholicism and the traditional Spanish 18th birth-day debut appeared in the ceremony.[49]

At the height of the debate in 1990, Rev. William Conway, writing for a Cath-olic Spanish-language audience, emphasized the actions of both Spanish missionaries and Mayans. In his article, Conway encouraged other Catho-lic clergy and laity to celebrate the event because it is the result of religious syncretism:

The *quinceañera* tradition has its roots in the cultural and religious practices of the Maya. Perhaps the great wisdom of the first missionaries that came from Spain to evangelize in the Americas was based on the ability to respect the culture and religious traditions of the indigenous population. Therefore, today we find a mixture of indigenous and Christian traditions. One example of this mixing is the celebration of the Day of the Dead.[50]

Instead of one civilization transforming another, he focuses on the syncre-tism of Catholicism and Mayan theology. Nevertheless, he constructs a ro-mantic mixing between Spaniards and indigenous populations, mystifying the way colonialism devastated most of the New World. In the end, Conway imagines *mexicano* culture in the same light as other clergy and journalists by placing the original (and therefore the presumed authentic) *quinceañera* in the ancient past. Ironically, these versions of the past include a model that views culture as porous and flexible, but they do not extend this model to the pres-ent and instead imagine that *mexicano* and "American" cultures are distinct, independent, and coherent.

MAKING A *QUINCEAÑERA*/MAKING THE SELF

My dissertation research was not designed as an exclusive study of the *quinceañera* but rather an investigation of the multiple displays of ethnic iden-tity. In many ways, I stumbled upon this form of expression in my field notes. As I prepared to write the dissertation, I found page after page detailing doz-ens of conversations about the *quinceañera*. In fact, one of my first field note en-tries describes a conversation with Victoria and several other *mexicanas* about her sister's *quinceañera*.[51] During a lunch break at the Spanish Coalition for Jobs (a federally-funded job-training center and my field site for the first eight months), Victoria described the details of each photograph to an interested group. A smaller group stood a few feet away and spoke under their breath about the old-fashioned celebration that had little meaning for women who want to have an "office job."

Taking the notes back into the field, I conducted structured interviews with twelve *mexicanas* and their mothers.[52] Those twelve were the *mexicanas* who consistently returned my phone calls and welcomed me into their homes; in other words, they were my closest friends. The group included *mexicanas* between the ages of eighteen and twenty-nine and their mothers (ages fifty to sixty-five, approximately); *mexicanas* who prefer Spanish and *mexicanas* who are monolingual English-speakers; and *mexicanas* with a G.E.D. and *mexicanas*, like Victoria, with some college education. The interviews were supplemented by participation in three *quinceañeras* and by an examination of photographs.[53] In fact, photographs became a point of entry for the discussions, as I would often begin by asking if they could show me their pictures of the latest *quinceañera*.

The field notes and transcriptions from the interviews include aspects of the *quinceañera* that are rarely mentioned in the public discourse. For example, young *mexicanas* spoke about the arguments they had with their parents over things such as the color of the dress, number of guests, or the location of the reception. This kind of parent-child conflict was missing in the public discourse. *Mexicanas* talked about the choreographed dance that might occur during the party. Older *mexicanas* spoke at length about the problems a family might face with particular clergy when trying to organize and coordinate a *quinceañera*. Most *mexicanas* spoke about the focus on the *Virgen de Guadalupe* during the service. A few mothers and daughters even discussed the option of taking a trip to Mexico or buying a car instead of celebrating one's fifteenth year. In general, *mexicanas* discuss a wider range of issues surrounding the *quinceañera* than clergy and journalists.

Although the *quinceañera* is described and practiced in several ways, mothers and daughters spoke most often about the *quinceañera* as "something that has to be done because of who we are" and as a way of "holding onto your roots." I interpret these expressions as an imperative to practice one's ethnic culture in an event that makes a girl into a woman, but more importantly makes her into a Mexican woman. However, the making of a *mexicana* is not an overnight transformation but an ongoing process and negotiation. Their own expression—becoming *conocido*—conveys the passage of time and relational process. The expression has at least two translations: becoming recognized as a woman and becoming known as a *mexicana*. "Becoming *conocido*" is a concept that focuses on the self, but it is not a compartmentalization of the self. It is an event that leads girls to discover and experience themselves as women, Mexicans, Catholics, and adults.

For one woman, whom I call Gloria, the *quinceañera* is an imperative because she believes that Chicago offers very few role models and even fewer opportunities to learn about Mexican culture. The event gave her daughter a sense of pride and self-worth as a *mexicana* in the face of local forms of discrimination and "assimilation." Gloria grew up in a parish that practiced segregation in the church and the classroom until the early 1970s. She experienced a history of institutional neglect that left many in her Back of the Yards neighborhood bitter and angry toward the Catholic Church. During a long interview at her home, she explained it to me this way:

Gloria: Because of who we are and because of who I wanted my daughter to be … my daughter's life has always been Americanized. We live here [in Chicago]. She went to school here. English is her first language, Spanish her second. So, how do you hold on to your roots? How do you put a value to it [if] you can't see it? … [It is] something that has to be done.[54]

In subsequent interviews, Gloria spoke about the *quinceañera* as an important time for a mother to encourage her daughter to become an independent woman. When I pressed her to clarify what she meant by an independent woman, she referred to her oldest daughter who had gone to college and was seeking a steady job. Gloria was proud that her daughter aspired to work in the media and did not pursue work outside of the Chicagoland area.

Although some *mexicanas* would agree with Gloria's reasons to celebrate the *quinceañera*, others would point instead to "our right" [*tenemos derechos*] to celebrate a girl's fifteenth year. Ruth, a mother who raised her ten children in Indiana, Illinois, and Mexico, argued that the Catholic Church has no right to stop these celebrations, and it was her "right" to perform aspects of her cultural heritage. Only one of Ruth's daughters, however, celebrated the *quinceañera*. According to her oldest daughter, Ruth refused this "right" for her daughters when money was tight, when daughters did not live up to her expectations, or when too many things were pulling the family apart.

Recalling her own *quinceañera*, Alicia, a young woman born and raised in Chicago, focused on the transformative powers of the event. Over lunch, Alicia described how she experienced her sexuality and cultural identity through the *quinceañera*.

Alicia: I just knew that a *quinceañera* was something that was very important to us. . . . It's something that a young lady should look forward to. I believe wholeheartedly that it's a step forward. Because I think that culture just makes you, not realizing that you are a woman. You have to make decisions as a woman, you know. When you are fifteen and younger you can be a kid . . . it's a step forward. It's saying it's okay to be a woman, it's okay to see those changes in any way it should be, mentally, physically, spiritually. It's kind of a jolt reaction . . . but it's good for you . . . 'cause otherwise I wouldn't know how or where the dividing point was in my life. I think the dividing point was there only because I actually thought and saw everyone together. After that I started losing weight like I said. When I look back I see that my life started at that point. After that, I am not saying right away when I turned fifteen, I am saying a couple of months later I started seeing that I like guys. For a long time I couldn't wear makeup … [Before that] I don't remember much except studying and school.

For Alicia, the event is experienced through a physical placement of one's body and begins the process of sexual awareness. Alicia's photographs from her *quinceañera* confirm her construction of a processual sexuality and cultural identity. For her first dance, Alicia danced with her uncle, not a boyfriend.

Victoria, a resident of the United States who never expects to return to Mexico, explained it to me this way: *niñas* become *jovenes*, but not *mujeres* [little girls become young women, but not adult women]. Using the combination of Spanish and English, the point is subtle but clear. The girl comes to experience herself as a sexual being, but not as a person who engages in sexual intercourse (or becomes pregnant).

Finally, a girl's heterosexual and religious identity is reinforced and constructed through the *quinceañera*. Many girls spoke about the *quinceañera* as the beginning of a personal relationship with the *Virgen de Guadalupe*: woman to woman, mother to mother, or woman to intercessor. According to Felicita, she, like many young women in her family, prayed everyday to the *Virgen*, a practice initiated after her *quinceañera*. The act of praying to the *Virgen* can be seen as a private moment in which *mexicanas* find their own voice. As Felicita once told me, "I talk to her about being a woman." Felicita and others not only found that women in their families developed a deep relationship with the *Virgen* after their *quinceañera*, but they also noted that most *mexicanas* wore a gold medal with the image of the *Virgen*. It stayed with them constantly, hidden under their clothes, but nonetheless physically near—an immediate reminder of their relationship with the *Virgen*.

The simultaneous creation and re-creation of their multiple identities through the *quinceañera* allows women to invent their own images of the *mexicana*. However, their construction of themselves is not based on carefree choices that produce harmonious images of whole *mexicanas* but instead leads to contradictory presentations of the self. For example, the event may be constructed as their entrance into womanhood and their desire to "improve" but the categories clash in unanticipated ways. Girls describe improvement as getting an education, an office job, or at least getting out of the factory. Improvement is future-oriented and illustrates a movement away from patriarchal gender roles. However, other future-oriented talk also includes a desire to find a boyfriend who won't beat you, who will support you, and who will not go to jail. Contradiction surfaces in their claim to the event as well. The argument that *mexicanas* have a right to celebrate their ethnic identity challenges local concepts of culture contact that encourage *mexicanas* to erase, hide, or forget their cultural identity and history. Nevertheless, *mexicanas* remake themselves through an event that is imagined as highly "traditional" within a patriarchal institution.

"JUST A TRADITION": CULTURAL MEANING AND AFFIRMATION

Though the *quinceañera* is framed as a "tradition," the category takes different meaning than the one constructed in the public discourse. *Mexicanas* do not value the *quinceañera* because they can locate its origins in a specific ancient civilization. Rather, they claim that the *quinceañera* is important because it transforms and physically connects a person to "Mexican culture"—a time and space that has particular meaning for each individual. Furthermore, mothers and daughters construct their version of the authentic *quinceañera* not by the form or practice of the event, but by the meaning behind or within the event. Since authenticity is located in meaning, it is not surprising that various forms and practices are referred to as a *quinceañera*.

Women spoke of "tradition" as a living practice in which innovation and continuity are not mutually exclusive. Objects, language, music, practices, and tastes need not have a traceable and unchanged precedent from the past. (This, of course, can infuriate scholars who devote careers to tracing the origins of cultural practices that they assume are passed down intact from generation to generation.) Adult *mexicanas* explain that the *"quinceañera* is just a tradition" that they locate in specific memories and family experiences. Following more than a temporal connection, most women link the *quinceañera* to a specific person, to a specific memory, or to a specific place—that is, to a sister, to *una quinceañera en el año pasado* [a *quinceañera* last year], or to the *rancho* of their childhood. Tradition can mean "What did sister do?" "What did *tia* [aunt] do?" The experiences of *padrinos*—members of the family either by marriage, birth, or sentiment—often play a significant role in tradition-making. In this way, "tradition" is a bodily experience authenticated by memory and practice.

When I asked women to describe the "most traditional" way to celebrate a *quinceañera*, they usually smiled tolerantly but disappointedly. Several contexts could produce their smiles. First, the facial expression can be understood as mutual positioning between researcher and participant. I was known to people as the Mexican whose research on "Mexican Culture" made me both an expert and a novice. Among women who attributed me with expertise, my questions about the *quinceañera* may have been perceived as a challenge to their own status. Or, they may have simply wished to defer to another person.

Second, some women might have smiled disappointedly because my question was too familiar. Many clergy who refuse to celebrate the *quinceañera* justify their actions by claiming that people do not know the "most traditional" way to celebrate the event. Therefore, my questions about the "most traditional" *quinceañera* could have led some women to believe that I agreed with their clergy. I suggest that underlying this kind of disappointed smile is a criticism of the Catholic Church.

Third, women were uncomfortable with a scale of "more or less traditional" because they saw the various forms of the event as an indicator of people's economic position. *Mexicanas* would not refer to a person as "less traditional" because she could not afford a fancy dress, a large reception, or a gold medallion. The forms of the *quinceañera* are directly related to one's economic position or the ability to solicit support from *padrinos*, who might pay for the cake, the photographer, the food, or any item that parents cannot afford. No one would describe the *quinceañera* of a family with fewer resources as "less traditional." As Nancy's mother told me, "It's just a tradition, but there was no money [for us to have one]." This view contrasts to that commonly held by anthropologists, journalists, and Catholic priests who routinely describe people as "more traditional" or "less traditional" by measuring attributes, characteristics, and behaviors. In this context, the smiling implies a challenge to the dominant narrative about traditionality, and it demonstrates a sophisticated analysis of the intersection between poverty and culture.

Fourth, nearly all women and girls would not allow me to generalize about the practice and form of the *quinceañera*. During interviews, *mexicanas* would not offer a definitive account of the *quinceañera*. They tended to disagree with my general description of the event, and sometimes there was considerable disagreement among family members. A daughter might claim that the dance was the important moment and her mother might claim that the church service was the important moment. They seemed to view the *quinceañera* as undefinable or beyond definition. I suggest that in their contestation, women and girls practice the negotiation of themselves, and they make negotiation an important aspect of the *quinceañera*.

This particular smiling and contestation, therefore, is based on the women's notion that culture can vary within one ethnic community. Their view of multiple identities is different from the dominant perspective of distinct "either/or" identities and nations. The popular narrative imagines people as members of homogeneous and mutually exclusive communities. Mexicans signaled through their smiles and contestation that people are never either Mexican or Americans but a hybrid form. Furthermore, this understanding of ethnic communities is itself a challenge to popular ideas about culture contact that assume that people are absorbed into the (imaginary) mainstream American experience. Finally, their ability to contest gender roles subverts the dominant view of a passive Mexican woman.

Another interpretation of this facial expression is illustrated in the following interview with Victoria, who despite the fact that she had organized her sister's *quinceañera* six months prior to our conversation claimed that she did not "know much" about the event.

Karen: I want to ask you . . . what do you know about *quinceañeras*?

Victoria: Well, I don't know much. The only thing I know is . . . it's that it's more like a tradition, it's just a tradition. . . . I don't know much about it. I wish I could help you. But I don't, I don't know 'cause it was just like a tradition.

Karen: Tell me about your experience.

Victoria: Okay . . . Well in church they do give you some kind of history about that, because they want you know what it's all about. I read my sister's [booklet] and what I understood was that it came, it started with French people. Funny too, French people. . . ? [W]hat it means is that a girl is turning from a little girl, a little girl is turning to a teenager, I guess. Not a teenager, like a . . .

Karen: A young woman?

Victoria: Older woman . . . what I remember from what I read, it said that it's like a girl is ready to get married. Once they do the cotillion [*quinceañera*] she's already like a woman.

Karen: Do you think that it's an important thing to do?

Victoria: My opinion, not really. I used to think so but then, I was talking to one priest and he made me change my mind . . . And I was talking about this one time and he said . . . "I think it would be just nice just to make a ceremony for her. And that's it. But why make all that party and those people?" He goes, "That's like saying, here's my daughter, like take her, like showing her off . . . Well, you're making a big party just because she's turning fifteen, like saying she's ready to get married. You know, here she is, take her." You know, that's how he put it . . . Then I started thinking, "Yeah, why make a big party when you turn fifteen. . . ?" [H]e says that he thought it was good to just make a ceremony for her. You know, and may be like, not a big party, but I guess like a family reunion and all that, but he didn't believe in cotillions. Something about the dresses too. He goes, "Why just waste all that money on that dress. Just put her in a nice dress." He was picky too . . . Well I guess they are blessing you and . . . See I know why I don't know, 'cause I'll ask my mom and she won't know what to answer me. I tell her. 'Cause I asked her, what does it mean. . . ? She says she doesn't know. But I have thought about it. And I cannot come up with an answer either . . . [E]verybody turns fifteen and they make a big party, that's the way I do see it. They make a big party. And it's like a tradition, you do it because other people do it, I guess. And because they, well, you know. I don't know . . .

Victoria expresses two important aspects of the *quinceañera*—gender and ethnic identity. First, people have different kinds of information about their own culture, in this case the *quinceañera*, that can seem incomplete and confusing (as with Victoria and her mother). "She says she doesn't know." Second, people's ideas about the event and their own gender and ethnic identity are dramatically shaped by the views of Catholic officials. I suggest that Victoria's expression, "I don't know," illustrates that ethnic identity is sometimes re-invented, confusing, and often imposed. Furthermore, Victoria's ability to plan, organize, and celebrate a *quinceañera* illustrates that she is not decultured, assimilated, or passive. Victoria, like many women, is able to create new ways of expressing and displaying herself when faced with uncertainty, unequal (but not determined) social relationships, or negative views of Mexicans.

DISCUSSION

This paper begins with my field notes about the events that took place before one *quinceañera* and explains to the reader that a general description is not forthcoming. It claims that a general description obscures diversity and an increasing contestation. More important, the paper argues that different explanations of the *quinceañera* are social analysis; that is, theories for experience. It then examines a wide range of ideas about the *quinceañera* and suggests that individuals have particular meanings of the *quinceañera* that are embedded in their understanding of ethnic identity, gender roles, sexuality, faith, and culture. The talk about the *quinceañera* is a discursive practice on the making of "*mexicana*."

For Catholic officials, the event, and therefore the construction of "*mexicana*," is grounded in another culture and another time, or perhaps beyond culture and outside of time. Catholic officials do not need to determine the place or time from which the event originates because they derive meaning from Catholic doctrine. They consistently claim that the event should be an expression of religious devotion and commitment to the church. The girl is encouraged to be subservient and to subordinate her wants and needs to those of her family and the church. Embedded within their image of a selfless mother/daughter is the codification of Catholicism's heterosexuality—delayed until marriage but nonetheless compulsory.

It is not surprising that the Catholic Church encourages this for women, but it is interesting that some clergy view alternate forms and practices—cultural sensibilities, if you will—as impurities from which they must "rescue" the *quinceañera* and their parishioners. Catholic officials who regulate the celebration claim they are saving *mexicanas* and their families from frivolously spending money or from focusing on social prestige and beauty. In 1990 Rev. Dahm publicly condemned the practice because he believed that the *quinceañera* is "just one big bash that costs an enormous amount of money, creates great indebtedness and brings no one to the churches." Dahm felt torn between maintaining a custom and promoting "materialism."[55] Rev. Raniero Alessandrini of St. Anthony Parish felt that the event was "a farce" because youth are "focusing on their appearance and the dinner that follows."[56] It is ironic that clergy in the Chicago Archdiocese, an archdiocese that between 1916 and 1929 organized one of the nation's most intensive Americanization programs for immigrants, currently discourage practices usually associated with assimilation. Why do Catholic clergy believe that extravagance dilutes a traditional practice? Why are they trying to save the *quinceañera*?

Perhaps their actions echo a classic motif of colonialism identified by Renato Rosaldo as imperialist nostalgia. Rosaldo argues that colonial administrators have a nostalgia for the culture they dominate and attempt to "rescue" traits of "the precious culture before it disappears forever."[57] Rosaldo's patronizing tone is deliberate because the "rescuer" rarely recognizes his own role in the destruction of the culture he longs to save.

Rosaldo does not acknowledge, however, that the liberal anthropological agenda of the late 1800s and early 1900s took a similar tone with Native Americans. American anthropologists, such as Franz Boas and Alfred Kroeber, saw their work among Native Americans as a "rescue mission" in the face of increasing culture contact and westernization. A fear of the end of traditional society and the vanishing primitive motivated Kroeber's work on Ishi, the last surviving Yahi Indian in California.[58] Despite cultural anthropology's rethinking of "the primitive" and rejection of nineteenth-century evolutionary models, the rescue motif persists. In fact, anthropology's attention to global capitalism often implies a prophetic warning of a disappearing object of study.[59]

It is important to clarify that I am not denying that aspects of culture (i.e., language) disappear as the result of particular encounters. The encounter between the New and Old World contributed to the disappearance of millions of people and their languages, practices, and customs. However, as James Clifford points out in his analysis of the rescue motif in anthropology, the problem with this framework is "the assumption that with rapid change something essential ('culture'), a coherent differential identity, vanishes."[60]

Catholic officials and journalists have imagined particular practices and forms of the *quinceañera* as essential aspects of *mexicano* culture. By identifying "something essential," they appear as advocates in the fight to save a vanishing tradition, a position that makes counterclaims appear ignoble.

"Rescue missions" in Chicago depend upon another anthropological convention. Catholic officials imagine *mexicano* culture as a self-contained and homogeneous unit that is distinct from the nation and culture of the United States. As Akhil Gupta and James Ferguson explain, anthropology tends to imagine distinct societies, nations, and cultures that correspond to divisions of space (i.e., national boundaries and political territories).[61] The assumption that space is discontinuous encourages anthropology students to specialize in geographic regions (i.e., Africa, Latin America, Asia) and not the spaces between them. When employed by Catholic officials and others in Chicago, this perspective allows people and practices to appear as if they originate from a single, independent culture.

Reclaiming and recreating ethnic culture, gender, faith, and heterosexuality in a cultural practice is a very different project than institutionalizing a ritual in the image of Catholic doctrine. *Mexicanas'* explanations for the *quinceañera* are grounded in an experience of dispersal that can produce ambiguous and conflicting meanings and practices. In Chicago, *mexicanas* encounter political and social institutions that promote, organize, and normalize assimilation through the erasure of their history or appropriation of their experience. Again Renato Rosaldo's work is helpful for understanding the process of cultural encounters. Rosaldo argues that all cultural encounters resemble a border-crossing experience because they can produce chaotic, confusing, and creative results. He borrows much of his argument from Chicana creative writers Gloria Anzaldúa and Sandra Cisneros, whose semiautobiographical works tell stories about crossing cultural, sexual, and other borders.[62] He argues that when two cultures collide, as they do in Chicago, people can find themselves in a "zone between stable places"—on unstable ground.[63] Instability can result from institutions that promote normalized identities (i.e., American and heterosexual) and informal processes that restrict historical memory. As social critics of assimilation, *mexicanas* "cluster around remembered or imagined homelands, places or communities in a world that seems increasingly to deny such territorialized anchors in their actuality."[64]

The *quinceañera* is an anchor between two cultures. It is a space in which *mexicanas* position themselves outside of and within dominant narratives about Mexican woman and the United States. First, the event publicly enacts and celebrates a culturally specific identity, a space in which *mexicanas* are positioned as social critics of the "melting pot"—that is, the event challenges the myth that immigration begins the inevitable process of shedding one's former culture.[65] They have avoided the inevitable by celebrating, defending, and contesting a "traditional" cultural practice. Second, the *quinceañera* borrows from practices and meanings found within the dominant culture. The two most obvious dominant narratives are roots and rights, motifs that have developed within "American" culture. Therefore, *mexicanas* create and participate in an event that contributes to their own assimilation.

Nonetheless, as Gloria Anzaldúa points out, *mexicanas* move through the uncomfortable territory, "this place of contradictions" between their Mexico and their United States, between patriarchy and equality in order to make sense of their lives.[66] It is a territory that permits two or more cultures, multiple meanings, and complicated constructions of a *mexicana*. It is a site of negotiation in which people and cultural practices are not coherent, whole, or distinct. The discourse and practice of the *quinceañera* encourage us to examine the paradoxical and ambiguous nature of "tradition." The discourse and practice suggest that what we intend as "cultural" is fluid, slippery, contradictory, spontaneous, and chaotic.

ACKNOWLEDGMENTS

The field research for this article was conducted from May 1990 to October 1992 among approximately forty *mexicanas* and their families. This work could not have been done without them. This paper benefitted from the comments of the anonymous reviewers at *Frontiers*. I would also like to thank Tamara Hamlish and the symposium participants at the American Anthropological Association 1992 Annual Meeting in San Francisco for their helpful comments on an earlier version of this paper. The research was funded by the Cushwa Center for the Study of American Catholicism at Notre Dame University, the Enders and Williams Fellowships from Yale University, and the Institute for Intercultural Studies.

NOTES

1. The term *mexicana* is the self-referent most commonly used by the women I met in Chicago. It should not be mistaken for an indicator of a person's nationality, length of time in the United States, or citizenship. Later in the paper, I more fully describe the *mexicanas* and their families.

2. *Quince años* [fifteenth birthday] is another, but less popular, term for the event. "*Quinceañera*" can refer to a person and to a thing (event). According to some Catholic leaders and a few *mexicanas*, "*quinceañera*" is Spanish for "cotillion," a formal ball or group dance. However, the Cordi-Marion Sisters and their Woman's Auxiliary distinguish between their own community-wide Annual Cotillion and the family-centered *quinceañera*.

3. For further reading on anthropology's cartography of insider and outsider see Elizabeth Enslin, "Beyond Writing: Feminist Practice and the Limitations of Ethnography," *Cultural Anthropology* 9:4 (Nov. 1994): 537–68; Akhil Gupta and James Ferguson, "'Beyond Culture': Space, Identity, and the Politics of Difference," *Cultural Anthropology* 7:1 (Feb. 1992): 6–23; and Stephen Tylor, "Post-Modern Ethnography: From Document of the Occult to Occult Document," in *Writing Culture*, ed. James Clifford and George Marcus (Berkeley: University of California Press, 1986).

4. Patricia Zavella, "Feminist Insider Dilemmas Constructing Ethnic Identity with 'Chicana' Informants," *Frontiers* 14:3 (1993): 58.

5. James Clifford, *The Predicament of Culture: Twentieth-Century Ethnography, Literature, and Art* (Cambridge: Harvard University Press, 1988); Renato Rosaldo, *Culture and Truth: The Remaking of Social Analysis* (Boston: Beacon Press, 1989).

6. Ibid., 19.

7. Ibid., 7.

8. Ibid., 147.

9. Gloria Anzaldúa, *Borderlands/La Frontera: The New Mestiza* (San Francisco: Spinsters/Aunt Lute Book Company, 1987); Gloria Anzaldúa, ed., *Making Face, Making Soul/Hacienda Caras: Creative and Critical Perspectives by Women of Color* (San Francisco: Aunt Lute Books, 1990); and Chandra Talpade Mohanty, "Introduction" and "Under Western Eyes," in *Third World Women and the Politics of Feminism*, ed. Chandra Talpade Mohanty, Ann Russo, and Lourdes Torres (Bloomington, Ind.: Indiana University Press, 1991), especially pages 66–74.

10. Mohanty, "Introduction," 29.

11. Octavio Romano-V., "Minorities, History and the Cultural Mystique," *El Grito* 1:1 (Fall 1967): 5–11; "The Anthropology and Sociology of the Mexican American," *El Grito* 2:1 (Fall 1968): 13–26; and Américo Paredes, "On ethnographic work among minority groups," in *New Directions in Chicano Scholarship*, ed. R. Romo and R. Paredes (La Jolla: University of California at San Diego, Chicano Studies Program, Chicano Studies Monograph Series, 1978).

12. Maxine Baca Zinn, "Field Research in Minority Communities: Political, Ethical and Methodological Observations by an Insider," *Social Problems* 27:2 (Dec. 1979): 216.

13. I do not intend to produce a romantic image of our reading together. As I expected, they did not agree with all of my interpretations of their words or ideas, and a few women did not respond to my phone calls and letters announcing that I would be in town for the summer. Nonetheless, each woman who received a copy of my dissertation (twelve in all) wanted to see and read her own words first. I eventually created an index for each woman so she could find herself/my representation of herself in my writing.

14. The most recent example of the Archdiocese's limited sensibility is their closing of St. Francis of Assisi, one of two *mexicano* national parishes established in the late 1920s. *Mexicanos* from the greater Chicago metropolitan area had been making St. Francis of Assisi the destination of pilgrimages since the mid-1960s.

15. See also Ruth Horowitz, *Honor and the American Dream* (New Brunswick: Rutgers University Press, 1983), 52–54, 243, n. 1.

16. Gwen Louise Stern, "Ethnic Identity and Community Action in El Barrio" (Ph.D. Dissertation, Northwestern University, 1976), 42.

17. Ibid., 43.

18. Ibid., 44.

19. Ibid., 5–6.

20. David Beard, "The Quinceañera: A Mexican Girl's Day as Cinderella," *Chicago Tribune*, 17 August 1980, section 12, p. 1ff. (italics in original). This article received wide circulation and was recommended to me by several Catholic priests.

21. Constanza Montaña, "Some Latinos Spare No Expense When Their Daughters Come of Age," *Chicago Tribune*, 19 June 1990, Metropolitan Section, p. 1ff.

22. The time under review (1971–1991) does not imply rigid periodization. Before the 1970s the Archdiocese of Chicago showed sporadic interest in the Mexican population. The analysis is based on an inventory of descriptions and explanations that surfaced several times and in different kinds of publications. Formal and informal interviews with Catholic priests, deacons, and nuns supplied additional information about the *quinceañera*.

23. In 1990 and 1991, the Archdiocese closed and consolidated over fifty-two parishes and schools. St. Casmir was consolidated with nearby St. Ludmilla in 1991 and renamed Our Lady of Tepeyac, a name that signifies the identity of its *mexicano* parishioners. St. Vitus was closed in 1990 but later purchased by a community coalition that is converting the building into a day care, arts, and neighborhood center for Pilsen.

24. Arturo Bañuelas, "La Tradicion de la Quinceañera," *Liturgy 80: Special Edition* 12:7 (Oct. 1981): 5.

25. Guillermo (William) Conway, "La Quinceañera: Segundo Articulo en una Serie," *New Catholic Explorer*, 5 October 1990, 20. Trans. by author.

26. Quoted in Lisa Holton, "Church Divided Over Quinceañera," *Chicago Sun-Times*, 18 July 1990, Business Section; p. 51; see also Arturo Pérez, "15 años Celebration" (unpublished manuscript, Chicago, Ill., 1990).

27. The Archdioceses of Los Angeles and San Antonio regulate the celebration of the *quinceañera*. Clergy in those cities are allowed to prohibit the event if worshippers do not fulfill certain prerequisites. Several parishes in the Archdiocese of Chicago have developed their own regulations based on the Los Angeles guidelines. Other Catholic officials in Chicago simply refuse to celebrate the event.

28. Holton, 51.

29. Ibid., 51.

30. Jorge Casuso, "Coming-out Parties Split Hispanics, Church," *Chicago Tribune*, 24 June 1990, 4C. See also Montaña, "Some Latinos Spare No Expense," p. 1ff.

31. Lisa Holton, "Tradition a Key to Hispanic Market," *Chicago Sun-Times*, 18 July 1990, Business Section, p. 47ff.

32. Bañuelas, 6.

33. Pedro [Peter] Rodriguez, "Los 15 Años: Rito Sagrado o Pura Pachanga . . . ," *El Puertorriqueño*, 21 August 1978[?], p. 10.

34. I suspect that the word comes from the British title for a male servant (chamberlain) and in Chicago it refers to male escorts. The female attendants are *damas*.

35. *Boletin, San Francisco de Asís* (Oak Park, Ill.: Claretian Missionaries Archives, March 21, 1971). Emphasis in the original. Trans. by author. From 1969 to 1976, Rev. Peter Rodriguez served as pastor of St. Francis of Assisi parish.

36. See Bañuelas; Laurie Hansen, "Hispanic Rite of Passage Seen as 'Teachable Moment' for Church," *New Catholic Explorer* 12 (Oct. 1990): 23; Pérez manuscript; and Pedro [Peter] Rodriguez, "Reflexiones," *New World*, 28 February 1975, p. 6.

37. Bañuelas, 5.

38. Ibid., 6.

39. Quoted in Beard, 4.

40. Rodriguez, "Reflexiones," 6. Trans. by author.

41. Ibid.," 6.

42. Quoted in Beard, 4.

43. Pérez manuscript.

44. Rodriguez, "Los 15 Años," 10. Trans. by author.

45. Bañuelas, 5.

46. Rodriguez, "Reflexiones," 6. Trans. by author.

47. Beard, 1. Ironically, a reference to Toltec civilization is rare, even though Chicago clergy extensively use Sister Angela Everia's guide for the *quinceañera*. Angela Everia, *Quinceañera* (San Antonio, Texas: Mexican American Cultural Center, 1980). In her guide she claims that the event originated in either the Aztec or the Toltec civilization.

48. Rodriguez, "Reflexiones," 6. Trans. by author.

49. Beard, 1.

50. Conway, 20.

51. The names of *mexicana* informants are fictitious in order to protect their privacy.

52. It was not my original intention to interview everyone's mother, but since several of my visits took place in the presence of mothers, I decided to include their comments as well.

53. This is probably faulty methodology for some anthropologists who emphasize observation over talk but I simply could not get myself invited to more than three celebrations. Though *quinceañeras* were celebrated three or four times every weekend

throughout the spring and summer and at nearly every *mexicano* parish in the city, ethical guidelines prevented me from observing these officially public events without a personal invitation. Instead, I take the words of *mexicanas* seriously and call for continued research.

54. Though Spanish is her first language, Gloria spoke to me in English during this interview.

55. Quoted in Montaña, "Some Latinos Spare No Expense," p. lff.

56. Quoted in Hansen, 23.

57. Rosaldo, 81.

58. Theodora Kroeber, *Ishi in Two Worlds* (Berkeley: University of California Press, 1963).

59. See for example, Susan Skomal's "Whither Our Subjects—And Ourselves?" *Anthropology Newsletter* 35:7 (Oct 1994): 1ff. Skomal introduces the newsletter's annual theme for the 1994–1995 academic year. Her article opens with questions about what will happen to the Lakalai of Melanesia by the year 2034. Skomal asks, ". . . will the sociocultural underpinnings that held the Lakalia have loosened beyond recognition?"

60. James Clifford, "On Ethnographic Allegory," in *Writing Culture*, ed. James Clifford and George Marcus (Berkeley: University of California Press, 1986), 113.

61. Gupta and Ferguson, 6.

62. Anzaldúa, *Borderlands/La Frontera*; Sandra Cisneros, *House on Mango Street* (Houston: Arte Publico Press, 1985).

63. Rosaldo, 85.

64. Gupta and Ferguson, 11.

65. Rosaldo, 81.

66. Anzaldúa, *Borderlands/La Frontera*, Preface.

The Power of Ritual in a Chicano Community: A Young Woman's Status and Expanding Family Ties

Ruth Horowitz

The *quinceañera* or cotillion, as it is sometimes referred to by Chicanos on 32nd Street in Chicago, is a celebration of a young woman's fifteenth birthday. It is found in many Latin American societies and today often involves an elaborate ceremony with large expenditures of money by many people. In Chicago many young Chicanos have masses and parties for as many as two to three hundred guests with two bands (Mexican and rock), drinks, and dinner. Relatives and friends are frequently asked to sponsor the occasion by paying for the girl's dress, the bands, the food, the liquor, the hall, and other small items. They are named as *compadres* (co-parents). Fourteen couples, *damas* (women) and *chabellanes* (men), from among the young woman's friends and relatives are invited to "stand-up" as escorts for the occasion and must pay for their matching long dresses and rented tuxedos. Outsiders might wonder why they spend so much money and incur debts to others when the average family makes considerably less than the national average. It is not, however, a potlatch or gaudy ball unconnected with anything in life with "no traditional or inherent reasons for being" (Rochberg-Halton 1986: 222) but is embedded in tradition, kinship, and community in a highly sophisticated money economy and powerfully provides meaning to several different audiences.

With the demise of traditional homogeneous rural societies and the growth of heterogeneous urban centers, many social scientists predicted the reduction of the importance of culture, ritual (Turner 1969), and primary relationships (Durkheim, 1964). Also there are consequences for social order (Toennies 1957; Wirth 1938). Some recent studies of urban communities argue that social order is constructed on the basis of territorial, age, sex, and ethnic segmentation of social groups (Suttles 1968, 1972), the complex division of

Ruth Horowitz: "The Power of Ritual in the Chicano Community: A Young Woman's Status and Expanding Family Ties," first published in *Marriage and Family Review*, vol. 19, issues 3–4 (1993): 257–80.

labor (Durkheim 1964), or a very weak culture created by the socioeconomic position of its adherents (Liebow 1967; Gans 1962). The conceptualization of social relationships in urban life in most of these studies is predominantly utilitarian, rationalistic, and instrumental. Behavior is seen as a means to an end. Networks are regarded as egocentric (Cohen 1974) and constructed out of need and relative power. This view of urban society largely relegates to the past and primitive, the importance of religion, rituals, and expressive symbols (Redfield 1941) in community life.

There is evidence that traditional rituals persist with modernization and high mobility rates (Dewey 1970; Carlos & Sellers 1972; Carlos 1973; Kemper 1982) and often co-exist with modern competitive economic relationships (Crumrine 1981). New rituals also develop in modern society (Burnett 1969). Specifically, there is some evidence that the *quinceañera* has become increasingly elaborate in modern urban Mexico (Kemper 1982; Nutini & Bell 1982) and is often partially financed by *compadres*. These sponsors become the young woman's *padrinos* (godparents). There are several more occasions in Mexico for which *compadres* are sometimes now named, such as burial, confirmation, and first communion, than just the traditional ceremonies of baptism and first communion, and more friends and neighbors are selected in place of relatives as *compadres* (Kemper 1982; Nutini & Bell 1980).

It is possible to view the *quinceañera* as an adaptation to economic and social marginality in a U.S. city. A utilitarian exchange view of social relationships might suggest that having a *quinceañera* increases the value of a young woman in the marriage market by parading her virginity and readiness for marriage publicly. That view also suggests that additions to the *compadrazgo* network merely extend or reaffirm the economic exchange network and that the family may be seeking status through demonstration of its ability to pay for a large affair in the community. In this view the *quinceañera* seems a rather outrageous expense as her participation rarely certifies a young woman's virginity nor does her behavior necessarily change as a result of the ceremony. It is possible to think of less expensive and more "rational" ways of expanding an economic exchange network or gaining status. While both economic exchange and "bride price" may contribute to an explanation of spending money on the *quinceañera*, it is only a small part of the explanation.

Secondly, the *quinceañera* is arguably a transitional phenomenon in the cultural sense inasmuch as it implies a need to affirm one's "Mexicanness" when one also feels that one is becoming somewhat Anglo. This implies that the more one's identity becomes firmly embedded socially and economically in the dominant culture, the weaker is one's attachment to ritual. The performance of the ritual would soon lapse. However, even as some Chicanos have become more embedded in the dominant culture, the *quinceañera* has remained a significant ritual, for example, among the middle class Texas Chicanos.

Finally, the ritual may also be viewed as urbanized traditionalism which stresses the dramatic presentation of cultural continuities of the past, despite the impact of the changes brought about by urbanization and immigration. This perspective both stresses the dramatization of the moral and symbolic boundaries that separate the Chicano community in the city from other ethnic groups and provides a basis to maintain that identity over time. In this view ritual does not necessarily disappear with increased integration into

American society. It may, however, take on new meanings and develop new forms. The *quinceañera* is best understood from this third perspective.

RITUALS AND THE PROCESS OF CULTIVATION

A collective ritual (secular or religious) is a drama staged as an attempt to bring an aspect of social life into orderly control, to structure social life (Moore & Myerhoff 1977; Myerhoff 1977). It is a ceremonial occasion of complex symbolic action and has several levels of meaning: some overt and others implicit. It may reiterate traditional social ties and provide integration for the social group (Durkheim 1965), but it also shapes culture. Moreover, ritual behavior is not just learned action that reflects the organization of society but "results from purposive interactions between individuals . . ." (Ford 1983). Symbols are living and changing entities. "In use and in experience, its meaning grows" (Charles Pierce 2.222: 302 as quoted in Rochberg-Halton 1986: 120) often more quickly than the entity itself. Consequently, rituals are subject to change (Duncan 1968) as people make decisions concerning how to do the ritual, its expense, and the meaning of the symbols. Unless the changes are collectively agreed upon by a group, the ritual may lose its collective legitimacy and symbolic significance. It may become hollow, its social and psychological power minimal;[1] not convincing its participants of its seriousness. However, the meaning of the symbols may vary among audiences as the meaning is constructed from the symbolic "object itself and from the perceptual apparatus of those who experience the object" (Griswold 1987: 1079).

While there is typically a specific purpose for a ritual, in this case, a public presentation of a young woman on her fifteenth birthday, as symbolic expression rituals do much more; they communicate both a social and moral order message (Manning 1977; Rappaport 1971).[2] Its form, formality, and repetitiveness surround the socially constructed meaning and make a dramatic statement about determinacy and against indeterminacy (Moore & Myerhoff 1977: 17). It stands apart from the annoyances and hassles of daily life and is more fixed. The question still remains as to how apart from daily life is the ritual and how is an elaborate ritual related to ongoing daily life?

Some focus on rituals as ways of facilitating the smooth continuity of daily interaction and constituting public interaction "where reality is being performed. The world, in truth, is a wedding" (Goffman 1959). Others focus on the ways rituals such as rites of passage and other ceremonial occasions are set off as dramatic events from everyday life. These latter studies tend to focus on the web of culture within the performance of the ritual without focusing on its production as part of daily interaction. A few studies such as that of Cohen (1980) link the politics of production of a London carnival to the drama of the carnival performance. Davis (1972) in his study of student nurses focuses on the drama of producing a ritual when one of the nurses becomes engaged. If we look at culture as a process and a medium in which we live (Rochberg-Halton 1986), we can begin to explore how elaborate rituals or ceremonies are connected to daily life which focuses our attention on the production of ritual as it has on the production of art and on why rituals are performed.

Meaning, in other words, is not simply a fixed and static realm "untouched by human hands," but has its existence in and through a process of cultivation, a process involving the development, refinement, or resultant expression of some object or habit of life due to care, inquiry, suffering, or celebration, and whose goal is the greater embodiment of living reasonableness. (Rochberg-Halton 1986: 114)

On another level symbols and symbolic action are essential to the development of self-hood. Identity is the meaning attached to self, its content and organization (Gecas 1973, 1982). The moral categories imbedded in the symbols form a basis for the social identities of the participants; they publicly and dramatically communicate that which distinguishes the group. Rituals provide a means to communicate "We are this kind of people and value those types of social relationships." The group is linked in the collective self that arises in the course of the experience of the transactions in the course of developing the production and performance of the ceremony (Mead 1974).

As both a rite of passage and intensification[3] it includes (1) symbols of the transition of the young woman into adulthood and (2) symbols of change or a reinforcement in the meaning of the relationship between the girl's family and that of all the sponsors. The ritual performance dramatizes the way things "should be" especially when compared to the process of preparation.

I spent three years as a participant-observer studying young people in the 32nd Street community (Horowitz 1986). I lived in the neighborhood for part of the study and attended several *quinceañeras*, sometimes as an uninvited guest brought by an invited guest and other times as a *madrina* (godmother). I spent much of my time talking with young women and men in their homes, on the streets, in the park, at dances, at private parties, at weddings, and in school. Conversations among the young women often turned to discussions of *quinceañeras* and "men."

AMBIGUITY OF PLACE

The position of the 32nd Street community relative to the wider society is complex, ambiguous, and marginal, both socio-economically and culturally. While the level of educational attainment and the value of the homes are among the lowest in the city, the median family income is higher than several other Chicago communities and the percentage of residents on welfare is lower than other neighborhoods of similar income levels. Moreover, the status of "Mexicans" in the U.S. is ambiguous. There is evidence that they are not discriminated against as much as blacks, yet they are not considered equal to Anglos and frequently were left out when federal resources were distributed to the blacks in the late 1960s and early 1970s (Horowitz 1983).

Outsiders generally categorically appraise the area as a slum in terms of its inner-city location. For example, urban residents often do not take advantage of the several superior local Mexican restaurants and pay much more to eat Mexican food elsewhere. Teachers rarely spend time in the neighborhood after school and the city has left many of the school buildings to deteriorate beyond repair.

The lack of social honor attributed to residents is not necessarily congruent with their own notions of social honor. Thirty Second Street residents desire to be viewed as respectable hard-working people. They do not regard their neighborhood as a slum and many renovated the interiors of their homes and worked hard to obtain federal and church funding for programs and services that the city failed to provide. The protests and proposals for improved educational programs and resources drew large numbers of residents.

Young residents, most of whom were born in the United States, generally view themselves neither as "Mexicans" nor "Americans." On the one hand, those who visit Mexico do not feel entirely comfortable and have little desire to live there. However, they desire to maintain an affiliation with that heritage and some of the traditions. On the other hand, they are neither viewed by others nor have they any desire to be viewed as "Americans." They are "Chicanos" or "Mexican-Americans," both of which names express their continuing marginal cultural and social position in the wider society. Community residents must resolve the problem of scarce resources, while, as Chicanos, maintaining their self-respect as hard-working people who help each other without depending on welfare institutions.

In the U.S. inner city there is little cultural or social support for the transformation from childhood to adulthood at fifteen or for traditional notions of purity and submission. On the one hand, there is little support for chaperonage. Both schools and community organizations have dances for those under fifteen with little chaperonage except perhaps for a brother. The media constantly shows younger girls dating, falling in love, and engaging in sexual relations. On the other hand, legally at fifteen, youth must remain in school and are treated no differently than before. They cannot leave home or marry without parental permission. Most residents are aware of the lack of support both in the community and the wider society for those expectations embodied in the *quinceañera*.

PRODUCING THE RITUAL: THE HEIGHTENING OF TENSIONS

Almost anyone who has been involved in the preparation of a wedding has experienced an increase in tensions among family members and between the bride and groom's families. Few brides survive the preparation stage without desiring to "eliminate" a relative, a mother, a mother-in-law, or the groom. The preparations heighten and openly expose and dramatize divisions, conflicts, and ambiguities in relationships. The interaction in the several months prior to the performance of the *quinceañera* more closely resembles that which Lewis (1951) found in Tepoztlán: conflicts, competition, mistrust, tension, and envy than the close ties described by Redfield (1930).

Tensions have plenty of time to develop as the planning must start many months prior to the event. The individual paying for the hall must put a deposit down; the young woman must choose and order the dresses after the fourteen girls whom she chooses to stand up with her are measured; they must order the engraved invitations, often from Mexico; they must plan the dinner and drinks; and they must hire the bands.

Not only can many things happen between the scheduling of the event and the event itself but many different people are enlisted to help out with the production of the affair. In addition to the expensive items such as the hall, the music, the liquor, and the dress, parents typically ask friends to become *compadres* and pay for the cake, the diadem, the flowers, an embroidered pillow, and often other small items. It is difficult to find fourteen girls who are willing and can afford to pay for the dresses, let alone finding fourteen male escorts. Families need to confirm the major sponsors and couples several months in advance as the names are printed on the invitations. During one *quinceañera*, a guest commented that the fourteen couples who were listed as "standing up" had probably never agreed to do so as only nine attended.

The economic realities of everyday life exert great pressure on social relations on 32nd Street. Some decisions resulting from shortages of funds can be a source of conflict among family members. Very few people have sufficient resources to meet all emergencies. For example, just before one *quinceañera*, the uncle who was to pay for the hall had to make a decision whether to attend the funeral of a relative who died in Mexico or pay for the hall. He and several members of his family went to Mexico and he backed out of paying for the hall three weeks prior to the event. The mother of the young woman fought with him and swore she would never help him out again. For several months they did not speak, but when he helped her out with something else, they reaffirmed the relationship. On other occasions, parents pulled their daughters out of the event because they found they could not afford to buy the *damas* dresses. While equal reciprocation is not expected, jealousy and anger are sometimes the result when one *compadre's* needs are met but not another's.

Tensions and conflicts between the generations and between traditions and current styles are also exposed. When one *compadre* who was to pay for one of the two hired bands dropped out, the mother insisted that only a Mexican band be hired. Her daughter did not want to go through with the plans for the event unless they hired a rock band. A day before the ceremony, they found one and someone to pay for it.

Additional problems include the loss of an escort because he and his girlfriend broke up or he was jailed. Hysteria prevails and everyone rushes around frantically to replace the lost escort. At the last moment the new recruit must rent a matching tuxedo. One young man refused to attend when he discovered that his tuxedo did not fit as he wished. Only when the young woman he was to escort cried, did he agree to go. All evening he kept asking me whether he looked all right. As this type of occurrence happens with some frequency, people become suspicious. On one level the image that emerges is that of a closely watched system of mutual obligations where each exchange is carefully monitored and weighed—a utilitarian, economically rooted relationship. On another level, the actual festivities and long-term relationships that evolve present an entirely different image. Becoming a *compadre* changes the meaning of the relationship.

Tensions also develop between the generations over the public behavior of the young woman. Rumors circulate about her virginity: If she spends too much time with a particular young man in public places then people become suspicious that she is too involved, but, if she is seen with several different men, then they think she is too free. Relatives report back to her family about her behavior. Arguments abound between the young woman and her family. On one occasion one young woman threatened to cancel her *quinceañera* a week before the event unless her mother would let her go out with her boyfriend to a dance that weekend. The mother gave in. Many of the young women talked about sneaking out to see their boyfriends during this period.

Sometimes arguments occur over whether to include a gang member as one of the escorts. Many of the gang members are valued escorts but parents are often worried that this will increase the possibility of fights at the party. This is a continuous problem as many extended families have a gang member among their members. Tensions often turn into open conflicts between the generations and family/*compadrazgo* relations over lack of resources and traditional versus current practices. Tensions and divisions which often remain tacit or submerged in daily life are heightened and dramatized during the production of the ritual.

AS A RITE OF PASSAGE: THE PERFORMANCE

Like the debutante party, the *quinceañera* publicly communicates that the young woman is no longer a child and that she is available for courtship. Unlike the distinct themes of each of the debutante parties, the *quinceañera* is conducted in a similar manner on most occasions. It does not express the individuality of each young woman as much as it communicates a collective link with tradition. It was not a major ceremony in small Mexican towns and the occasion was often distinguished only by a young woman receiving a new dress and shoes (Lewis 1951). The *quinceañeras* on 32nd Street generally have more symbols of a young woman's change in social status, many of which concern sexual purity and dependency on men. She goes from being a child (a nonsexual person) to being a sexual being, but, most importantly, an untouched one. She is no longer free to play openly in heterosexual groups and must constrain her presentation of self so that no one questions her purity while finding a husband. She must present herself as available but not as desirable in the sense of an object of passion. Until the wedding her life is full of danger and tension. When she becomes a sexually active person the ritual both indicates the dangers and suggests a way to resolve the tensions.

The rehearsals, the formal adult attire, the procession, and the choreographed dance at the beginning of the party provide an atmosphere of dignity and restraint and enshroud the occasion with importance. The young woman dresses in a long white dress, her escorts wear matching evening attire, and her immediate family buys new clothes for the event. All rehearse the procession into the church for the mass, the order in which her *padrinos* present her with gifts during the ceremony, and the specific pattern of the waltz performed prior to dinner. Everything must proceed according to plan.

On the day of the *quinceañera*, the fourteen couples, several of the *padrinos*, and the young woman on the arm of her father march down the church aisle for mass and communion. The young woman kneels in front of the priest, usually alone but sometimes with her young escort (a boyfriend or a relative). During the ceremony her new *padrinos* present her with gifts; an embroidered pillow for kneeling, a diadem, often jewelry, and flowers for offering at the shrine of the Virgin. The young woman goes alone during the ceremony to the Virgin's shrine, gives her the roses, and thanks her for being allowed to celebrate this joyful occasion and for receiving so much help and pleasure from her family. The entire group takes communion before everyone files out.

The ceremony with its pageantry and its beauty allows the emotional involvement of both the participants and the observers. Many of the women cry and the men look uncomfortable. Typical comments after the ceremony are "wasn't that beautiful," "I've never seen one so lovely before," or "she looked so beautiful and grown up." Everyone is clearly moved by the event.

That evening she is formally presented to all the guests when she enters the hall on the arm of her father. First she dances with her father who then presents her to her escort and then her escorts dance in a specified pattern. One young woman spent several days teaching her friends the pattern of the dance, while others hire someone to do so. According to Nutini and Bell's (1980) study of Mexico, this is supposed to be the first time she dances, marking her entrance into the adult world. This is not typically true in Chicago. After dinner and photographs, she dances again under the careful eyes of her relatives. Her formal adult attire, her dance in front of an audience are juxtaposed on the childlike behavior of many of the younger guests who run, play under the tables, and dance in groups.

The essential ritual elements concern purity, adulthood, attractiveness, and male supervision. Purity is the key. The young woman wears white, her father lingers close by, and she prays to the Virgin. Unlike a wedding ceremony, there is little overt recognition of her sexuality, she does not remove and throw a garter, no one throws rice, and she does not toss a bouquet to the other young women. While she has an escort, they rarely share or exchange anything or feed each other cake that would link then symbolically. In fact, sometimes a relative escorts her.

Symbols of sexuality and passion are excluded, yet she is a sexual person in that she is presented as available by making her as attractive as possible, but not as an object of passion. Nothing is held back in attempting to enhance her beauty: the long white dress, new jewelry, hair done in an intricate, sophisticated style, and make-up applied with a practiced touch. She is the center of all attention for one evening.

While she is supposed to be entering adulthood, she is not supposed to become increasingly independent. Her father never gives her away during the evening without reclaiming her. All generations attend and are supposed to chaperone her until her marriage. While others may go to an after-hours bar after the party, she never does.

The ritual dramatizes how she should behave as an unattached young woman and indicates the importance of doing it properly. Managing one's presentation of self as an attractive, demure young woman is critical during the next stage of her life. She should not be flashy in dress or demeanor nor overtly claim center stage. Everything must be handled with subtlety and formally as demonstrated in her presentation of self at the *quinceañera* and in the reactions of others.

CULTURAL IMPACT

While the ritual may not convince everyone of the individual woman's virginity, it is successful in shaping the culture. Purity remains important in giving meaning to personal actions even though some young women do not remain virgins until marriage, a seeming contradiction. Without the coercive control of chaperonage, young women are faced with a cultural dilemma (Horowitz 1983): remain virgins (bounded sexuality) or give in to their boyfriends who are supposed to dominate women and who desire premarital sexual relations, an open expression of passion (unbounded sexuality).

Many young women seek to maintain the "boundedness" of their sexuality while engaging in sexual relationships. This can be done by explaining that in a moment of heated passion they gave in to their boyfriend, which is also correct behavior, that is, no premeditation that use of birth control permits. Bounded sexuality (purity) as opposed to an open expression of passion remains possible but the activities have changed (Horowitz 1983). The symbol of virginity, therefore, has limited direct behavioral consequence. No one knows if she is a virgin or will remain one. The public acknowledgment of the importance of a young woman's continuing purity through "chaste" actions as an adult is dramatized as is the past and future collective efforts of the family network to affect an appropriate transition to adulthood. Thus, the ritual cannot be explained as the public affirmation of an individual's state. However, it both points out and provides a solution to the tension of remaining an untouched sexual person until marriage. It does provide the symbolic and moral boundaries that distinguish this group from other urban groups and continues to help maintain that identity even as behavior changes and the young women become increasingly integrated in the wider society through participation in schools and popular culture.

THE PERFORMANCE AS A RITE OF INTENSIFICATION

While the mass provides the sacred aspect of the ritual, the party afterwards is more concerned with dramatizing community and family. It ritually repairs the backstage tears in social relations and links past to present while providing additional symbols of the link between the young woman and her family and among community members. Upon their arrival at the hall, the guests typically place their gifts on a central table where the many tiered white cake is displayed. After the waltz the women serve dinner, often chicken *mole* (a spicy Mexican dish) with rice, beans, and tortillas. The family makes an effort to maintain the Mexican quality of the affair; however, integration into the dominant culture has at times impacted upon the symbolic links to Mexico: they sometimes serve U.S. food and hire U.S. rock bands.

If the family serves fried chicken, guests sometimes comment about its appropriateness. One of the guests complained in a very nasty tone "you would have thought that they would have taken the time to make *mole*." After the young woman cuts the cake, the dancing begins in earnest. Often two bands play—one Mexican and one rock. While this indicates that integration affects some aspects of the event, it does not mean that there is less attachment to the ritual.

The interaction during the party resembles that found in Tepoztlán by Redfield (1930): joyful, cooperative, and spirited. Everyone arrives dressed up and prepared to have a good time. A variety of residents attend: all ages, upwardly mobile people, friends and relatives, young and old, males and females, gang members and nonmembers, family and friends. Entire families are invited including small children, and it is not unusual to bring an extra relative or friend. The *damas* and *chabellanes* bring their families. Typically several gang members attend; however, they do not wear their colors and usually refrain from getting into trouble even when enemy gang members are present. While relatives and close friends make up the core group of guests, invitees generally extend well beyond this more narrowly defined group. Sometimes people attend who have just heard about the party.

The dancing, drinking and gossip often continue well past midnight when most guests drag themselves home. A large number of photographs of the escorts, friends, and family capture the happy memories and, when guests visit, the family brings out the album. Pictures of the young woman often adorn the living room walls along with graduation and wedding photos. The success and joyfulness of the occasion can be reaffirmed frequently. The audience, in this case the guests and family members, can joyfully affirm the importance of the moral and symbolic significance of the event, symbolically repairing some of the tension and danger of relationships in everyday life.

COMPADRAZGO AND CONFIANZA

Asking friends and relatives to help sponsor the affair obligates the family to several others for significant favors. On the one hand, incurring debts for a party seems almost foolhardy when the *quinceañera* as a rite of passage has so little impact on actual behavior. The money might be used more "rationally" to pay for school, fixing the house, or food. On the other hand, making many of one's friends *compadres* and asking relatives to become *compadres* adds a dimension to or reinforces the relationship by dramatizing it. The help of others makes it possible to have such extensive ceremonies that allow for collective expressions of solidarity and normative statements concerning social relations.

Becoming a *compadre* and the obligations and responsibilities that it entails are different than those incurred by friends and neighbors involved in exchanges in daily life. Exchanges among neighbors and friends make daily life easier and relieve some of the pressures of inner-city life. They borrow small amounts of money, exchange food, provide child care, or locate jobs. Each favor is returned as rapidly as possible with one of equal value, that is, a state of balanced reciprocity (Sahlins 1972) exists. For example, one family sent complete meals for a week to a friend when the husband was in the hospital and had no compensation. He painted the family's house when he felt better. These exchanges are carefully monitored and a relationship is terminated if a loan is not repaid. Being without resources for a considerable period is sufficient to be evaluated as a loser and most efforts to help out by nonfamily members are terminated. One gang member who constantly invited himself to others' homes for dinner without reciprocating was finally told that he ought to get food stamps. This was a very insulting comment because he would have to depend on the state, which publicly indicated that he had no friends or family, a less than honorable situation.

Participating in the success of a party says something publicly about the relationship. By contributing to a symbolic event, it symbolizes a change or reaffirms the nature of the relationship of the young woman's parents and the sponsors. They participate largely because of the nature of their relationship, not out of economic necessity. Participation is a statement concerning the trust or confianza[4] between relatives or compadres. "Confianza designates generosity and intimacy as well as personal investment in others; it also indicates a willingness to establish such generosity and intimacy" (Velez-Ibanez 1983: 11).

Becoming a sponsor by contributing extensively to a largely symbolic event is a statement that communicates, first, that the girl's parents have sufficient confianza in the sponsors that they think will follow through on their obligations and second, that the sponsors have sufficient confianza in the girl's family that the relationship will continue. Haas and Deseran (1981) refer to this as "investment in expensive gestures of good faith" (12) that are symbolic exchanges. The extensive giving in the "sponsor" relationship has a different meaning than the gift giving (Caplow 1982: 391) of the Middle-towners' among relatives at Christmas which "is a method of dealing with relationships that are important but insecure. Gifts are typically offered to persons or collectivities whose good will is needed but cannot be taken for granted" (1982: 391). That kind of gift giving more closely resembles in the quinceañera the giving of a gift (a sweater, a blouse, or a record) to the girl by the invited guests.

The social consequences of the public statements concerning new relationships in the social network should be a change in the nature of the exchanges from balanced reciprocity to generalized reciprocity (Sahlins 1972) and for some, a restatement of generalized reciprocity. Exchanges can he much greater in consequence and need not be fulfilled rapidly or equally. Large loans may be made, a child may be taken in for a considerable period, or a job may be obtained through the relationship. One family sent their pregnant fifteen year old daughter to a compadre in another state. No money changed hands and when the daughter returned, the compadres kept the baby along with their own five children. One gang member after he was involved in a serious shooting, stayed with his padrinos and their six kids in another state without contributing to the family income. When asked about returning the favors one man responded "When he needs me, he knows I'll help his family."

In the honor based subculture, indebtedness is a symbol of dishonor, so that only as *compadres* are large debts not experienced as dishonorable. Social relationships no longer hinge so much upon material exchanges but material flow is sustained increasingly by social relationships. The meaning of the network is changed and/or reaffirmed and community members can say that they are the kind of people who can help each other and need not rely on outsiders. Unless the use of welfare can he explained as a result of an extreme emergency, it is regarded as dishonorable to use it. When one man was locked out of his job, he suffered enormously but refused to ask for State assistance and would take food only from his union which he regarded as mutual aid among equals.

The young woman begins to build ties to her new *padrinos*, but there is nothing within that relation that makes it necessary. The young woman begins to develop an exchange network with her friends through the outlay of money for the dresses. She is obligated to stand up for the *quinceañeras* of the others, if they should ask. One young woman stood up for six in the year following her own.

THE JUXTAPOSITION OF PREPARATION AND PERFORMANCE

The tensions of preparation heighten and separate daily life from the performance of the ceremony. Daily life appears reasonably calm and orderly compared to the period of preparation, even if the orderliness of the ceremony is never achieved in daily interaction. The presumption of order remains intact though there are always disruptions in everyday interaction: parents fight with their daughters, daughters get pregnant, relatives and *compadres* are not always prepared to help out when needed, and gang members hurt each other and sometimes bystanders, even during an event such as a *quinceañera* or wedding. Community members can assess what the actions of others mean, even if things do not work out as planned.

Symbols that Distinguish the Community

Having a *quinceañera* does not distinguish the young woman from other young women, or her family from other families as qualitatively different kinds of people. Whereas, there is an exclusive and official list of who can have a debutante party and can "come out" at an official ball, a family can have a *quinceañera* if the girl is not yet a mother or visibly pregnant. The *quinceañera* along with several other occasions symbolically links the generations and members of the community. It does not distinguish some residents from others as different kinds of persons. While some parties may receive more applause than others for giving a more expensive or beautiful party, it does not set off that family as a different kind of family from others in the community. Any family that is able to take care of its debts and helps others is respectable. The *quinceañera* is just one of many occasions to make new *compadres* or to reaffirm old relationships.

Many young women on 32nd Street do not mark their fifteenth birthdays. If a family gives a *quinceañera*, often only one sister has one. Some young women have big weddings instead, but few have both. If one looks at all the ritual occasions for which *compadres* can be added to the network, one sees that most families have a number of possible occasions to do so. Most families have baptisms for each child, the occasion when the *padrino* relationship is considered most important. Typically, for other affairs, the *compadre* relationship is more salient than the *padrino* relationship. *Compadres* may be added for first communions, graduations, and weddings (Kemper 1982; Nutini & Bell 1980).

The intensity of the family network allows the celebration to occur and it is through the *quinceañera* that these relationships are publicly dramatized so that the extent and intensity may be evaluated. The more expensive and extensive the party, the more praise received. While the close scrutiny given the *quinceañera* by participants and outsiders alike may help a family gain the respect of their community, the process also engenders competition as to the relative strength, loyalty, extensiveness, and wealth of family networks. Should the liquor run out or the food fail to measure up, people talk about the family. At one party complaints were registered when the liquor ran out before midnight or a family may be criticized for having fewer than fourteen couples escorting the young woman. One young woman who had only thirteen couples commented that it was much better than the seven at the *quinceañera* of a friend the previous week. It is the strength of family network that is evaluated.

Comparisons are made by everyone in attendance. Moreover, with the generally limited resources of all local residents, everyone is aware that competition will continue among network members for each other's favors. The *quinceañera* and *compadrazgo* affirm the moral solidarity of network members who claim to have similar virtues. However, competition over scarce resources increases the rivalry among network participants and those who have a *quinceañera* gain some social status. Only by participating in this relationship, accepting its norms and obligations, can people expect and enjoy the benefits of the relation.

As a cultural event, the *quinceañera* presents messages and symbols that serve to gloss over and obscure the competition and ambiguities of everyday life. It communicates a continuity with the past while masking the changes, discontinuities, and conflicts of traditionally Mexican and U.S. urban ways of life. *Compadrazgo* symbolically changes the meaning of social relationships and in doing so disguises the reality of the need to divide and sometimes compete for small resources. It allows community residents to maintain their self-image as independent hard-working respectable people, while often depending on others for daily needs. Now that many 32nd Street residents are born in the U.S. and some prefer to use English over Spanish, some do not feel as comfortable in Mexico as they might wish and see themselves as being different. The use of *compadrazgo* as a central symbol links 32nd Street Chicagoans to their Mexican past as does the serving of Mexican food and the printing of invitations in Spanish. The *quinceañera* allows people to see themselves as respectable and independent with a heritage of which they can be proud in a world that often does not offer them respect and denigrates their past by trying to make them into "Americans." While the ritual has become more Americanized and meets new needs in the U.S., it still remains important and its tenacity cannot he explained solely by the lack of integration in the U.S. society.

IRONY AND URBANISM

The symbols in the *quinceañera* continue to fire, to evoke emotion and joy among the participants. It is not a ritual empty of meaning like so many found in modern America (Klapp 1969). In the ritual there is a shared feeling and experience of solidarity and emotional life, most of which is not linked directly to the social and economic marginality of the Chicano in U.S. cities, nor is it merely a transitional cultural phenomenon, a result of the Chicanos' lack of integration into the dominant culture. One must not underestimate the continued symbolic and moral importance of the *quinceañera* despite and because of the dislocations of immigration and urban life. It is unlikely to disappear regardless of the structural position of Chicanos. In fact, it allows and creates a means of remaining distinct from the dominant culture, while integration continues within the socioeconomic system.

While the exigencies of everyday life often tend to foster conflict and competition, the *quinceañera* as ritual communicates something different. On one level *compadrazgo* symbolizes a certain type of social relationship and the ritual communicates its importance and extensiveness within the community. The ritual and all its trappings, both the sacred and community, communicate that it is important for a young woman to remain pure and remain in control of her passions until marriage. She must remain demure and attractive—a potentially long period of danger and often not entirely navigated successfully.

On another level, how the various audiences perceive what is communicated is not necessarily the same while it symbolically links those audiences. Unlike the Durkheimian argument concerning the reaffirmation of common sentiments in rituals and the univocal nature of symbols, the power of the ceremony also rests on the multi-vocality of its symbols. On this second level, the meanings attached to the ritual by different groups—the adult men as fathers or male relatives and the adult women as mothers or female relatives are distinct. To the adult men, the fathers, this traditional route is the route they would like their daughters to follow, that is, to preserve the aura of innocence and femininity that goes with purity and which allows them to remain in control of the timing and occasion of their daughters' sexuality; a church wedding with her purity intact.

To adult women, the mothers, the girl going through the ceremony is an idealized image of what they would like to have—the power that comes from purity. While women are supposed to be submissive, they are not, in a cultural sense, passive. In the cultural logic of the situation, going through the ceremony, regardless of whether the girl is actually a virgin, confers upon the person who successfully negotiates the difficult straits the glory of someone who has wrested the sacred (the church) and community (the party) validation from the envious, though supportive, crowd.

Here is where there is a curious reversal. The ceremony appears increasingly extensive today because both the urban fathers and mothers have a common symbolic interest that is under control and largely taken for granted traditionally—that it is quite rare for a girl to remain a virgin. Rumors abound prior to and after the ceremony; some of which have validity.

The third audience, the youth, tend to mess things up. And it is precisely because in real life the ambiguity is strongly felt that there is a need for an ideological resolution of what is absent from the ceremony symbolically. The need is to demonstrate the proper order of dominance and control between the generations. The point of the ritual is to show the younger generation what is supposed to happen—daughters are supposed to listen to their fathers and sons are not supposed to seduce daughters, so that one cannot tell a virgin from her opposite. The fact that everyone is so acutely aware that there is a fairy tale quality to the event underscores its message. In the proper order of things, kids do, in fact, do what their elders tell them they ought to do regardless of the circumstances. On the one hand, it should not be surprising that in a community that stands in an ambiguous relation to the wider society and one in which males and females each have their own social world and in which the ties between the generations have become more ambiguous, that the ceremony has different meanings for each of the audiences. On the other hand, the very ambiguity in the symbols allows the ritual to remain powerful for each audience and to provide strong links among them.

The ritual may for the greatest part be understood as urbanized traditionalism. It stresses continuities of rural Mexico—purity, *compadrazgo* and more minor symbols of the past: food, language, music, invitations, and sometimes either decorations or jewelry given to the young woman. These continue their importance despite significant changes brought about by urbanization and immigration—no chaperonage, better jobs, availability of social services, and the U.S. youthful styles of male-female interaction. In spite of the increasing structural and cultural integration into the dominant society, the *quinceañera* communicates strong moral and symbolic boundaries that separate the Chicano community from other communities. This does not mean that there is no utilitarian value to having a *quinceañera*. When economic resources are limited, a certified pure young woman may be in a better position to obtain a husband and *compadrazgo* facilitates necessary economic exchange. In fact, those in some middle-class communities tend not to rely so heavily on *compadres* to finance the event.

At present it is difficult empirically to determine the degree to which the *quinceañera* arises from the ambiguities of the cultural situation of Chicanos. While Chicanos are becoming more integrated into the dominant culture, they experience their lives as neither "American" nor "Mexican." It is not clear as they become increasingly integrated whether the ritual will become meaningless and then abandoned. This does not, however, appear to be a realistic assessment. If the ritual is performed to communicate moral and symbolic differences from the wider society and the performance itself symbolically reinforces these differences, it will remain as long as people desire to maintain those differences even if the ritual changes.

NOTES

1. "Operational effectiveness" is, according to Moore and Myerhoff (1977: 12), social psychological effectiveness, not doctrinal efficacy. The operational effectiveness of a rite is an empirical question: whether the ritual was a success or failure at accomplishing what it was supposed to do or to communicate.

2. There is also an indexical aspect of ritual; however, this will not concern us here.

3. According to Chapple and Coon (1942), a rite of passage "restores equilibrium in a system that after a crisis involving an individual" (507), while a rite of intensification focuses on the group that requires some change in interaction. It reinforces prior relationships. Here it changes and intensifies the meaning of the social bond that links the members of the network.

4. *Confianza* is a term used frequently in Mexico and among Chicanos to designate this type of social relationship. For a discussion of *confianza* in a Mexican marginal community see Lomnitz (1977) and for one among credit union participants in the U.S. and Mexico see Velez-Ibanez (1983).

REFERENCES

Burnett, J. 1969. Ceremony, Rites and Economy in the Student System of an American High School. *Human Organization* 28 (1), 1–10.

Caplow, T. 1982. Christmas Gifts and Kin Networks. *American Sociological Review* 47 (June), 383–92.

Carlos, M. L. 1973. Fictive Kinship and Modernization in Mexico: A Comparative Analysis. *Anthropological Quarterly* 46, 75–91.

Carlos, M. L., and Sellers, L. 1972. Family, Kinship Structure and Modernization in Latin America. *Latin American Research Review* 7, 95–124.

Chapple, B. D., and Coon, C. 1942. *Principles of Anthropology.* New York: Henry Holt and Company.

Cohen. 1974. *Two Dimensional Man.* Berkeley: University of California Press.

Cohen. 1980. Drama and Politics in the Development of a London Carnival. *Man* 15, 65–87.

Crumrine, N. R. 1981. The Ritual of the Cultural Enclaves Process: The Dramatization of Opposition Among the Maya Indians of Northwest Mexico. G. P. Castile and G. Kushner (eds.), *Persistent Peoples.* Tucson, AZ: University of Arizona Press.

Davis, F. (ed.) 1972. Rituals of Annunciation. *Illness, Interaction and the Self* (pp. 39–57) Belmont, CA: Wadsworth.

Dewey, A. G. 1970. Ritual as a Mechanism for Urban Adaptation. *Man* 5 (3), 438–48.

Duncan, H. 1968. *Symbols in Society.* New York: Oxford University Press.

Durkheim, E. 1964. *Division of Labor in Society* Trans. G. Simpson. Glencoe: Macmillan.

Durkheim, E. 1965. *The Elementary Forms of the Religious Life.* Trans. J. W. Swain. New York: Free Press.

Ford, G. 1983. Za Dusha: An Interpretation of Funeral Practices in Macedonia. *Symbolic Interaction* 6 (1), 19–34.

Gans, H. 1962. *The Urban Villagers.* New York: Free Press.

Gecas, V. 1973. Self-conceptions of Migrant and Settled Mexican Americans. *Social Science Quarterly* 54 (30): 579–95.

Gecas, V. 1982. The Self Concept. *Annual Review of Sociology* 8, 1–33.

Goffman, E. 1959. *The Presentation of Self in Everyday Life.* New York: Anchor.

Griswold, W. 1987. The Fabrication of Meaning. *American Journal of Sociology* 92, 1077–1117.

Haas, D., and Deseran, F. A. 1981. Trust and Symbolic Exchange. *Social Psychology Quarterly* 44 (1), 3–13.

Horowitz, R. 1983. *Honor and the American Dream: Culture and Identity in a Chicano Community.* New Brunswick: Rutgers University Press.

Horowitz, R. 1986. Remaining an Outsider: Membership as a Threat to Research Rapport. *Urban Life* 4 (4), 409–30.

Kemper, R. V. 1932. The *Compadrazgo* in Urban Mexico. *Anthropological Quarterly* 55 (1), 17–30.

Klapp, O. E. 1969. *Collective Search for Identity.* New York: Holt, Rinehart and Winston.

Lewis, O. 1951. *Life in a Mexican Village: Tepoztlán Restudied.* Urbana: University of Illinois Press.

Liebow, E. 1967. *Tally's Corner.* Boston: Little, Brown and Company.

Manning, P. K. 1977. *Police Work.* Cambridge: M.I.T. Press.

Mead, G. H. 1974. *Mind, Self and Society.* Ed. C. Morris. Chicago: University of Chicago Press.

Moore, S., and Myerhoff, B. 1977. Secular Ritual: Forms and Meanings. In S. Moore and B. Myerhoff (eds.), *Secular Ritual* (pp. 3–24). Amsterdam: Van Gorcum.

Myerhoff, B. 1977. We Don't Wrap Herring in a Printed Page: Fusion, Fictions and Continuity in Secular Ritual. In S. Moore and B. Myerhoff (eds.), *Secular Ritual* (pp. 199–126). Amsterdam: Van Gorcum.

Nutini, H. G., and Bell, B. 1980. *Ritual Kinship.* Princeton, NJ: Princeton University Press.

Rappaport, R. A. 1971. Ritual Sanctity and Cybernetics. *American Anthropologist* 73 (1), 59–76.

Redfield, R. 1930. *Tepoztlán.* Chicago: University of Chicago Press.

Redfield, R. 1941. *The Folk Culture of Yucatan.* Chicago: University of Chicago Press.

Rochberg-Halton, B. 1986. *Meaning and Modernity.* Chicago: University of Chicago Press.

Sahlins, M. 1972. *Stone Age Economics.* Chicago: Aldine-Atherton.

Suttles, G. 1968. *The Social Order of the Slum.* Chicago: University of Chicago Press.

Suttles, G. 1972. *Social Constructions of Communities.* Chicago: University of Chicago Press.

Toennies, F. 1957. *Community and Society.* New York: Harper and Row.

Turner, V. 1969. Forms of Symbolic Action. In Spencer (ed.), *Forms of Symbolic Action,* (pp. 3–25). Seattle: Washington University Press.

Velez-Ibanez, C. 1983. *Bonds of Mutual Trust.* New Brunswick, NJ: Rutgers University Press.

Wirth, L, 1938. Urbanism as a Way of Life. *American Journal of Sociology* 44, 3–24.

From Church Blessing to Quinceañera Barbie®: America as "Spiritual Benefactor" in La Quinceañera

Kristen Deiter

Feliz Cumpleaños, Barbie doll! This doll celebrates the time-honored Hispanic tradition of *Quinceañera*, which celebrates a girl's special 15th birthday. Doll comes with tiny presents and a picture frame. Available as Hispanic or Caucasian doll. Suggested Retail: $14.99. Available in May. (*2001 Dolls: New Barbie® Doll Releases*[1])

It endures as the best-known metaphor for the United States: America is a melting pot to which people from diverse backgrounds come and meld into Americans. In this process of melding or assimilating, though, America's ethnic groups often lose their histories, customs, and languages—indeed, their very cultures and identities. This loss occurs, in part, because America as a host culture or dominant culture modifies its ethnic groups' religious traditions. Mindful of this phenomenon, I spent three years studying one American ethnic group and its religious practices: in 1996–97 I worked full time at a large Hispanic Catholic Church in San Antonio, Texas, and for the next two years I taught the predominantly Mexican-American or Chicano students in that city's Catholic high schools. Throughout the study, I conducted a survey of my students' views and observed and talked with Latino Americans of all ages in the Hispanic or Latino American neighborhoods where I lived, worked, and worshipped. In these settings, I witnessed the evolving spirituality of many Latino Americans as a result of their acculturation as Americans, particularly concerning *la quinceañera*,[2] one prominent Latino socioreligious tradition that, according to Michele Salcedo, is gaining popularity in the United States.[3]

Kristen Deiter: "From Church Blessings to Quinceañera Barbie©: America as 'Spiritual Benefactor' in *La Quinceañera*," first published in *Christian Scholar's Review*, vol. XXXII, no. 1 (2002): 31–48.

A Catholic term used in this essay may call for definition: sacramentals. "Sacramentals are associated with or imitate the Church's official rituals. . . . They include religious signs, symbols, public and private devotions, prayers, gestures, rituals, music, images, and natural or made objects. . . . In themselves they may not be religious. . . . They become sacramentals and, therefore, sacred, in their religious purpose and use."[4] With this term in mind, we may investigate America as "spiritual benefactor"—a term I use ironically because a number of "beneficiaries" object to some "bequests," and because some other "bequests" actually harm the "beneficiaries."

Erich S. Gruen has introduced this "benefactor/beneficiary" metaphor to represent the power that a host culture wields over its immigrants and their descendents:

> . . . the tracing of cultural influences from one society to another . . . generally presupposes a rather passive recipient, thus posing a distinction between cultural benefactor and beneficiary. . . . I refer to the manipulation of myths, the reshaping of traditions, the elaboration of legends, fictions, and inventions . . . with the aim of defining or reinforcing a distinctive cultural character.[5]

In this case, through its Catholic Church and popular culture, America has become not only the "cultural benefactor,"[6] but also the "spiritual benefactor": the Latino-American immigrants to this country and their descendents, the "spiritual beneficiaries."

A HISTORICAL "SPIRITUAL BEQUEST" TO LATINO AMERICANS

To illustrate, this "spiritual benefactor/beneficiary" relationship has recurred throughout American history, notably since the 1920s, when the United States received a mass influx of Mexican immigrants who retained many Old World religious traditions.[7] Working in the parish office of a Hispanic Catholic Church in San Antonio, I sometimes encountered these traditions, particularly the blending of Mexico's Spanish and Indian religious practices.[8] For instance, Latinos occasionally came to the parish office, requesting gallons of holy water to fill their trucks' radiators to keep the vehicles from breaking down. (According to *Catechism of the Catholic Church*, blessed water and a prayer are a sacramental used to sanctify objects,[9] such as homes and religious articles—the Church does not sanction the use of holy water as a truck fluid.) Besides presenting priests with teaching opportunities, requests like these exemplify the lasting emphasis that many Mexican-American families placed on sacramentals. Generally, these families kept *altarcitos* (family altars),[10] and individuals made supplication to a saint as a *manda* or *promesa* (promise). When the prayer was answered, the people made an obligatory pilgrimage to that saint's shrine or completed another promised task.[11] They also believed in evil spirits and trusted spiritual *curanderas* (healers) to protect them from the spirits.[12]

Through the years, these religious traditions have concerned many American priests who considered *mandas*, *promesas*, and *altarcitos* to be superstitions.[13] In 1965, 94 percent of priests polled demphasized these forms of popular piety, fearing that they made the Catholic Church in America appear "ridiculous."[14]

Although the Church venerates the saints, some American priests believed that Mexican Americans took it too far, and some priests, who felt threatened by the *curanderas*, preached against them.[15] The Catholic Church in America, therefore, has acted as a "spiritual benefactor" to Mexican immigrants and their descendents, conforming their spirituality to the style of Catholicism practiced in the United States. In fact, "In 1949 the Priests Conference for the Spanish Speaking for the Archdiocese of San Francisco reported, 'Among the people there is widespread superstition, even the practice of witchcraft.' [This] had to be eradicated if the Mexican Catholic was to fit the American Church."[16]

LA QUINCEAÑERA—A QUARRY FOR "SPIRITUAL BENEFACTORS"

More recently, both the Catholic Church and American popular culture have assumed the role of "spiritual benefactor" with respect to the *quinceañera*. The word *qinceañera*, in most Latino cultures and in this essay, refers to both the custom itself and its honoree.[17] Norma E. Cantú calls the *quinceañera* "a living tradition" and "an ever-changing organic performance"—particulars having been added onto it or "fallen by the wayside" throughout the years,[18] and details varying by family custom and geography. Still, the following explanations create a general impression, which I will refine shortly. Susan Orlean defines the *quinceañera* as: "a ceremony that takes place when a girl turns fifteen years old (*quince* [fifteen] *años* [years]), [which] celebrates her passage into womanhood, her commitment to Catholicism, and her debut into society."[19] It consists of a Mass "at which the girl is blessed and is asked to affirm her dedication to the Church" and, afterwards, a party "at which she is introduced into society and celebrates her birthday."[20] Dale Hoyt Palfrey specifies, "The celebration is a way to acknowledge that a young woman has reached sexual maturity and is thus of a marriageable age."[21] And Ruth Horowitz corroborates Palfrey's point: "[The *quinceañera*] goes from being a child (a nonsexual person) to . . . a sexual being, but, most importantly, an untouched one. She is no longer free to play openly in heterosexual groups and must constrain her presentation of self so that no one questions her purity while finding a husband."[22]

Regarding the origins of this rite of passage, speculations abound. The Duchess of Alba, in eighteenth-century Spain, has been credited with starting the *quinceañera* custom when she invited adolescent girls to the palace and dressed them up as women. In the nineteenth century, the Empress Carlotta of Mexico likewise presented her court members' daughters as young ladies eligible for marriage.[23] On the other hand, Valentina Napolitano describes a similar rite of passage practiced in ancient times by Toltecs and Aztec warriors: "Girls who undertook the celebration were ready to be chosen by a male of the tribe and taken to the mountain. Soon after, they became pregnant for the sake of 'community' reproduction."[24]

Significantly, despite the similarities among these customs and the *quinceañera*, Cantú proclaims that the *quinceañera's* source is unknown: "Although it appears obvious that the origin of the *quinceañera* lies in a syncretism between the Spanish court dances and the native Mexican (Aztec and other Amerindian) initiation rituals, there is no conclusive evidence to suggest any particular origin."[25] Napolitano confirms this fact: Even in Guadalajara, Mexico (that nation's second largest city), the source of the *quinceañera* is not known. Elderly women there do not recall celebrating the tradition (though middle-aged women do), and because the *quinceañera* is not a sacrament, church records of the celebration do not exist. "The first reports of the feast started to appear in the *Sociales* (social events) section of Guadalajara newspapers during the early 1940's";[26] incidentally, a published memoir also indicates that the first known *quinceañera* was celebrated in the United States (specifically, in Laredo, Texas) in 1941.[27]

Consistent with Cantú and Napolitano's research is the view of Elly Moran, an expert in Hispanic Cultures, particularly *sincretismo religioso* (the blending of religious and folk/cultural tradition). Decades ago in Mexico, she says, the *quinceañera* was a social celebration of a young woman's ability to bear children and consequent readiness for marriage. Parents would tell their daughter, "We present you as a *señorita* into society," and shortly thereafter, the daughter was expected to marry and have children.[28] Thus, whatever its origins, by the mid-twentieth century in Mexico, the *quinceañera* had become primarily a social celebration—not a religious one.[29] It was celebrated in the Church only because parents could not present their daughters to society otherwise: "Belonging to the Church made them upstanding members of the society."[30] Cantú seems to agree, asserting that the intrinsically communal nature of any Latino celebration necessitates that it include a religious component.[31] Hence, today most Latinos, being Catholic, seek to have a private Mass celebrated in the *quinceañera's* honor.[32]

THE CATHOLIC CHURCH IN AMERICA AS "SPIRITUAL BENEFACTOR" IN *LA QUINCEAÑERA*

But the Church has questioned its own celebration of a girl's sexual maturity at the age of fifteen. With the number of teen pregnancies declining but still precariously high, some Anglo priests have criticized the *quinceañera's* emphasis on a teenaged girl's sexuality, and some have censured it as "advertising a young woman's sexuality."[33] This has actuated the Church, as "spiritual benefactor," to redefine the *qiunceañera*, assigning to the rite a new, Christian meaning.

As an illustration, in *"Tienes 15 Años* (Now That You Are 15)," Father Mark J. Brummel, C.M.F., attributes the *quinceañera* not at all to court dances, but only to indigenous fertility rites, and then emphasizes adolescent girls' fertility from a different perspective. He writes,

> For many ancient agricultural cultures, the most important thing was the creative force of nature. Many divinities in those cultures represented life-giving elements such as earth, water, and sun. Fertility was associated with women and many communities celebrated the moment at which a young woman became capable of giving birth.
>
> This celebration assured the community of its continuity, because life would be passed on. It was important for the community that a girl make a commitment to serve the community and help to insure its future.

The ritual of initiation of the young girl as an adult member of the community was also an affirmation that the whole community was in right relationship with the divinities and with the order of nature and the world.[34]

This prefaces his explanation of the Church's teaching on the *quinceañera*: "Christian communities have appropriated these rooted traditions. When a young Hispanic woman turns 15 the whole community joins her to give thanks for her life and to witness her commitment to serve the community and to be faithful to her beliefs in the future with full responsibility as an adult."[35] Emphasizing responsibility to the community, rather than sexual maturity, Brummel names the special achievements of eight influential Hispanic women in the United States who have committed themselves to public service in their communities[36] and therefore serve as role models for *quinceañeras*. And he directly addresses adolescent girls, again stressing abstinence and community service: "Fertility means something more than the ability to have children. You are probably already physically able to have children, and yet it is too early for you to do so. . . . But it is not too early to respond to the call of your community."[37]

In *Quince Años: Celebrating a Tradition: A Handbook for Parish Teams*, Sister Angela Erevia, M.C.D.P., concurs with Brummel: "The *quince años* tradition is rooted in the history, traditions, and celebrations of our ancestors with Hispanic and indigenous origins."[38] Then she lists the ancient, indigenous religious traditions that centered on birth, childhood, and initiation rites at puberty, and compares them to Christian traditions at the corresponding stages of life.[39] Yet, having read Erevia's comparison, Cantú insists, "Although it is easy to see a relationship, I find it difficult to trace a direct link between the [indigenous religious traditions and the *quinceañera*]. . . . All of [Erevia's] conjectures are ultimately just that, and there is no evidence to suggest a root origin for the [*quinceañera*] tradition."[40]

Nevertheless, in these educational texts, Brummel and Erevia ascribe the *quinceañera* to the indigenous rites alone—minimizing the sexual nature of the rites[41] and ignoring their synthesis with other, purely social, celebrations of a young woman's readiness for marriage. In ways like these, the Catholic Church has reshaped the *quinceañera*, bringing the tradition's meaning in line with Catholic teachings, most likely to justify the Church's continued celebrations of the *quinceañera* Mass. In fact, according to Sister Rosa María Icaza, C.C.V.I., the *quinceañera* is a sacramental.[42]

AMERICAN POPULAR CULTURE AS "SPIRITUAL BENEFACTOR" IN *LA QUINCEAÑERA*

The Church has not single-handedly altered the meaning of the *quinceañera*; rather, another "spiritual benefactor," American popular culture, has proven at least as influential as the Church in changing this tradition. Years ago in Mexico, Moran says, "the *quinceañera* was a farewell to childhood." At the *quinceañera*, for the last time, the girl wore a pink dress, her hair in large, spiral curls, "like a baby, a kid." She received her last doll (as she does to this day) and had her last childhood portrait taken, posed on a swing. Even throughout most of the twentieth century, until the the girl turned fifteen, she neither wore makeup, panty hose, high heels, or perfume, nor was she allowed to dance with boys or to have a boyfriend. The message was: "You're a baby; you're still a girl."[43] But, as Latino Americans become more assimilated, the custom evolves.[44] Currently in the United States, the girl wears white to her *quinceañera*, and she dresses as a woman.[45] In fact, she wears a white, lacy, floor-length gown,[46] often made of satin and indistinguishable from a wedding gown. One *quinceañera's* aunt even said, "I think her mother's praying that Maria keeps her figure, so she can wear the dress again when she gets married."[47]

Quinceañera gowns now demonstrate "both the effects of Americanization on taste and a certain American-style expansiveness about price"[48] and only begin to reveal the extent to which American popular culture has commercialized the *quinceañera* celebration. Indeed, the wedding industry in the United States is a big business, one that has tapped into a new market in the growing number of Latino Americans celebrating *quinceañeras*. From 1980 to 1990, for example, the Hispanic population in Phoenix, Arizona, increased 65 percent, and near downtown Phoenix, the *quinceañera* business at "Aztec Plaza, . . . the biggest formal wear shopping center in the world, . . . enjoyed a corresponding upswing."[49] Monica Humbard's aptly titled article, "Minority Marketing Equals Major Sales Opportunities: Expand Your Sales Base by Reaching Out to Ethnic Customers," offers demographic information on the U.S. Hispanic population and then outlines techniques for florists to use when marketing to Hispanic families, who, for *quinceañeras*, "spend an average of $2,000 on flowers alone."[50] And any cursory search for "*quinceañera*" on the World Wide Web results in hundreds of hits for wedding-related American businesses that likewise advertise their exquisite (and expensive) *quinceañera* goods and services. Because American popular culture bombards Latino Americans with images that blur the boundaries between traditional American weddings and *quinceañeras*, girls and their families necessarily dream about, plan, and celebrate their *quinceañeras* under the media's influence, further empowering the advertisers. A cycle consequently seems to develop, every year the wedding industry marketing the *quinceañera* more vigorously to a client base that, under the industry's power, plans fifteenth birthday celebrations that resemble lavish weddings. In fact, a closer look at the whole *quinceañera* event in America demonstrates its similarity to a traditional American wedding.

Just as a prospective bride and groom begin their wedding plans by setting a date, usually at least a year in advance, so do the *quinceañera* and her family. In Mexico, the *quinceañera* customarily takes place on the girl's fifteenth birthday; however in the United States, as most weddings do, it generally takes place on a Saturday.[51] Then, while the engaged couple considers everything from newspaper announcements and a color scheme to invitation styles and printers, from menus and banquet halls to fabrics and dress designers, so do the *quinceañera* and her family,[52] they may even hire a wedding consultant.[53] In addition to the *quinceañera's* gown, the family selects teenaged couples to participate in the ceremony and chooses dresses and "headpieces for the girls . . . tuxedos . . . for the boys."[54] They choose "photographer, a videographer, table decorations and favors for the guests—even a limousine."[55] They hire "entertainment—strolling musicians, *mariachis*, or [a] disc jockey,"[56] and order a cake. "The most elaborate cakes are made up of several decorated layers that sit atop columns and connect to the main cake by bridges . . . which span a fountain bubbling with colored water. Fresh flowers decorate the cake, and on the top, a *quinceañera* may stand in front of a lace fan. The whole thing can cost several thousand dollars. . . ."[57] And, as stated, they order flower arrangements: "corsages for [the girl's] mother and grandmothers; boutonnieres for her father, her grandfathers, and the *chamberlán de honor* (honor escort); wrist corsages or small bouquets for the *damas* (young ladies in the court of honor), and even flowers on their headpieces. . . ."[58]

As a traditional American wedding begins with a religious ceremony, a typical *quinceañera* begins with "a Mass in Spanish."[59] At the church, the *quinceañera* looks like a bride, attended by her groom, bridesmaids, and groomsmen. Indeed, like a wedding party, the court of honor sometimes includes one or more flower girls.[60] Monica Ortega writes that the *quinceañera* usually pairs her twenty-eight closest friends or relatives into fourteen couples, each representing one year of her life, who precede her down the aisle at the ceremony as her court of honor. She and her honor escort, her closest male friend, make fifteen.[61] Father Arturo Perez, an expert on popular Latino expressions of faith, has led the *quinceañera* preparation program at St. Roman Church in Chicago. He explains that the *quinceañera's* parents escort her down the aisle during the Processional Hymn that begins the ceremony, and her date escorts her during the Recessional Hymn afterwards "as a way of highlighting her change in status. . . . She comes in with her parents, but she leaves with this young man."[62] While a couple takes marriage vows at their wedding, the *quinceañera* often renews her baptismal promises during her rite.[63] Throughout the ceremony, like a betrothed couple does, the *quinceañera* kneels in front of the priest, sometimes with her escort.[64] The new spouses make a public commitment to one another; likewise, "The *quinceañera* may make a public commitment to her family, her faith, her education, and her chastity."[65] And, like a newly married Catholic couple presents flowers to the altar of the Virgin Mary at their wedding, the *quinceañera* presents 15 roses to the same altar at her ceremony.[66]

Also like a wedding, the *quinceañera* church service is followed by a reception for as many as two to three hundred guests[67] who, upon arriving at the hall, place their gifts on a central table where the many tiered white cake is displayed.[68] There, the court of honor is introduced and the *quinceañera* presented.[69] Then, after the toast, dinner, and formal thank you, with the court of honor seated at the head table[70] like a wedding party, the *quinceañera* cuts the cake,[71] and the dancing begins "with the *quinceañera* dancing with her father, usually to a waltz. She continues to dance with her father for the second number and her escort dances with her mother. Halfway through that song they switch, so the *quinceañera* is dancing with her escort and her parents are dancing with each other."[72] Ortega's explanation of this ritual alludes to the wedding tradition of the bride's father giving away his daughter: the *quinceañera's* father "hands [her] over to dance with [her] escort."[73] "For the third number, the rest of the court joins in. . . . Family members [may also] . . . have a solo dance with the *quinceañera*,"[74] like a bridal dance.

Likewise similar to a large wedding, a *quinceañera* of this magnitude creates a tremendous expense. The party "could take several years to finance. . . . *Quinceañeras* in Miami are legendary in extravagance and can top six figures in cost."[75] And there is a reason for the expensive reception. As Salcedo addresses the girls and their families: "The reception is the moment you have dreamt about [and] waited, worked and planned for. . . . The presentation, that magic moment when *la quinceañera* is presented as a young woman to her guests, is the dramatic high point of the evening."[76]

American popular culture, particularly the media, cultivates this emphasis upon the reception. The September 1997 issue of *Latina Bride* (again, the wedding industry targeting the *quinceañera* market), for example, features two articles on the *quinceañera*. The first, Ortega's article, discusses four *quinceañera* traditions, two that take place at the reception and one that culminates there.[77] The other article lists 38 steps for planning a *quinceañera*. A few times it mentions the ceremony and officiant but never God, the Church, religion, or faith.[78] By glorifying the *quinceañera*'s social elements and discounting or ignoring its spirituality—the reverse of the Church's approach—American popular culture acts as a negative "spiritual benefactor," detracting from and vitiating the celebration's religious significance.

I attended a *quinceañera* as an invited guest and found the sacred and secular aspects of the tradition to be in conflict, two forces of American culture contending as "spiritual benefactors." Faith was definitely a value, evidenced by the seven full-page Mass program, which provided the lyrics to all of the hymns, every word of the Scripture readings, and all of the prayers and responses. The invitation likewise stated that the *quinceañera* would "come before God, the Almighty to offer thanks for the life he has given [her]" and called the church ceremony "the religious celebration of [her] Fifteenth Birthday" and "a Holy Mass" at which she would express [her] feelings before God on becoming a young lady." However, the next page of the invitation demonstrated less spirituality and more worldliness as it labeled the girl not as *Quinceañera*, but as *Debutante*; noted in boldface: "Wishing Well Available"; and listed the girl's sponsors—relatives and family friends who had helped defray the cost of the celebration by paying for the services or items (such as the limousine or the *quinceañera*'s high-heeled shoes) listed alongside their names. Erevia defends this list of sponsors from a religious standpoint, calling it a "litany" that shows the extended family's involvement in the celebration and their love for the *quinceañera*.[79] Even so, when parents called the parish office where I worked, desiring to plan their daughters' *quinceañeras*, they most often referred to the celebrations as *debuts* (likening them to "debutante balls, where the daughters of the social elite are presented in ostentatious displays of wealth"[80]), as this invitation indirectly did, influenced by society's secularizing the tradition.

Clearly, the *quinceañera* "take[s] on new meanings and develop[s] new forms ... with increased integration into American society."[81] Moran laments, "Today there is so much contamination—loss of identity from blending with other cultures."[82] In fact, "From a north-of-the-border viewpoint, [the *quinceañera*] may be seen as a cross between [a] Sweet Sixteen and a debutante's coming out party . . . [due to] the relentless onslaught of *gringo* culture prevalent today. . . ."[83] Note Salcedo's diction, for example: "The tradition may be to debut at fifteen among Latinos, but the North American influence is having an effect. In the Northeast, many Latinas put their *quinceañera[s]* off a year and call [them] . . . Sweet Sixteen[s]."[84] To debut at a religious celebration creates a natural conflict between the secular and the sacred features of the event. Yet, as Salcedo later uses the term *quinceañera/debut*,[85] many San Antonians likewise speak of "debuts," "*quinceañeras*," and "Sweet Sixteens" interchangeably. Perhaps because of these various terms for similar celebrations, which include parties but not necessarily religious facets, Americans tend to emphasize the social facets.[86]

THE CHURCH'S REACTIONS TO POPULAR CULTURE AS "SPIRITUAL BENEFACTOR" IN *LA QUINCEAÑERA*

Indeed, America's social influence over the *quinceañera* has frequently counteracted the goals of the Catholic Church. First, the Church "frowns upon" attempts to make the celebration resemble a wedding.[87] Second, "The media constantly shows younger girls dating, falling in love, and engaging in sexual relations,"[88] which denies the Church's teaching on chastity, emphasized at the *quinceañera* Mass. And third, because many *quinceañera* receptions are excessive and the rite's religious aspect is largely ignored,[89] some priests feel the *quinceañera*'s meaning is lost.[90] Priests have complained of prospective *quinceañeras* who know nothing of the rite's sacred meaning and never even attend Mass; who expect to celebrate the tradition "even if they [are] pregnant or [are] using drugs"; and who pester their parents into throwing extravagant receptions.[91] In fact, for these reasons, some priests debate whether to celebrate the rite at all.[92]

In an attempt to redress these problems, the Catholic Church in America, as "spiritual benefactor," has further changed the *quinceañera* tradition. Several parishes and some entire dioceses have promulgated requirements that a girl must meet before she may schedule her *quinceañera* Mass.[93] At the parish where I worked in San Antonio, for instance, prospective *quinceañeras* were required to have received the sacraments of Baptism, Reconciliation, and First Eucharist and either be in at least their third consecutive year of C.C.D. (Confraternity of Christian Doctrine) classes or be enrolled in a Catholic school. Each prospective *quinceañera* was also required to participate in a one-day parish *Quince Años* Preparation Program which included reflecting upon the religious meaning of the celebration (especially the commitment to chastity) and planning her *quinceañera* Mass. Catholic Church officials justify these changes as their endeavor "to reclaim . . . traditions, which have become secularized in the United States. . . ."[94] We're trying to make sure the religious significance is maintained," said Father Frank Rossi, chancellor of the Galveston-Houston Diocese. "With the church blessing comes the expectation of Christian living."[95] Specifically, Sister Juanita Martinez, who has taught *quinceañera* classes at St.

Ann's Roman Catholic Church in Houston, "also teaches a class on sex; education and on 'how to say no.'"[96] In the words of Perez: "[the *quinceañera*] allows
us to talk about sexuality in real positive terms before everybody. . . . It gives us
an opportunity to say to [the *quinceañera*] and the girls in her court, 'You hold
power in this community.' Because that's what sexuality is about, in a lot of
ways. How will they use it? For good? Or not for good?"[97] And the Church aims
to demphasize the inordinate spending that has come to characterize *quinceañera* celebrations because, Martinez notes, sometimes "the parents invest a lot
of money. After the [*quinceañera*] you discover the phone is disconnected and
they're over here in the social ministries for help to pay rent and bills."[98]

The Catholic Church's *quinceañera* preparation programs are gaining popularity. In the Diocese of Phoenix, Father Antonio Sotelo, the bishop's vicar
for Hispanic affairs, has written a guidebook for *quinceañeras*, in which he ad-
vises that the girls study the Bible, Latino-American and *quinceañera* history,
and morality, and attend a retreat with their parents.[99] And Father Roberto
Broccatto, Associate Pastor of the Sacred Heart Parish in San Jose, California,
promotes group celebrations of the *quinceañera* Mass, in which several fifteen-
year-olds from different families are honored together in a jointly celebrated
quinceañera.[100] He organizes mini-retreats for his parish's *quinceañeras* and
their families to learn the Church's attitude toward the celebration and to encourage the families' participation in the parish community. In fact, his parish does not offer separate Masses for individual *quinceañeras*. Pleased with
the results of his program, Broccatto reflects, "Before they went through the
program of preparation at the mini-retreat, I think they saw the Mass as an
opportunity to dress up and show off. . . . I hope that the attitude of thinking
of the Mass as the main thing of the *quinceañera* becomes more widespread."[101]
Father Jimmy Drennan of San Antonio reports that the Church's stance on the
quinceañera is indeed becoming more widespread: ". . . Father [Broccatto] . . .
has taken a different approach, as [have] many other churches throughout
our nation and different parts of Latin America, that the *quinceañera* is . . . no
longer just the celebration of a young woman, but it is the celebration of an
entire parish community. . . ."[102]

As "spiritual beneficiaries," Latino Americans have mixed feelings about
the Church's *quinceañera* preparation programs. Some families, often the needy
or recent immigrants, resist the Americanization because they are still attached
to the way the rite is celebrated in Mexico.[103] To be sure, I often spoke with
parents in San Antonio who, upon learning the stringent requirements of the
parish where I worked, chose to celebrate their daughters' *quinceañeras* at other
parishes that took the religious preparations less seriously. For some of these
families, the *quinceañera* maintains their separate identity and affirms their
"Mexicanness" when they are "becoming somewhat Anglo."[104] "[It] allows
people to see themselves as respectable and independent with a heritage of
which they can be proud in a world that does not offer them respect and denigrates their past by trying to make them into Americans."[105] And some wealthy
Hispanics resist the group *quinceañeras* because they want their daughters to
have private ceremonies.[106] Yet others embrace the changes, among them Caroline Coronado and her daughter, Alice Coronado Hernandez, who has chaired

a group *quinceañera* in Phoenix. "We're really happy with doing our *quinceañera* the way Father Sotelo has suggested," Caroline said. "We felt that the classes and the retreat were really good for the girls. We saw what was going on with the *quinceañeras*—we saw the problem out there. Even if we could afford it, we knew it wasn't good to continue the old way."[107]

ONGOING "BEQUESTS" FROM THE TWO "SPIRITUAL BENEFACTORS"—AND SOME CONSEQUENCES

As "spiritual benefactors," both American secular society and the American Catholic Church continue to take the *quinceañera* in new directions. Instead of traditional *mariachi* music following the waltzes, for instance, modern American music has become the norm,[108] and the families sometimes serve American food instead of traditional Mexican dishes.[109] Additionally, "In many places across the country and in Puerto Rico, groups of *quinceañeras* are presented to society."[110] These celebrations include the Cordi-Marian Cotillion in Chicago, celebrated as a Mexican debut; the annual *Quinceañera* Ball in Zapata County, Texas; the Symphony Debut in El Paso;[111] and the Vesta Club *Quinceañera* Ball in Phoenix,[112] which calls its honorees *debutantes*.[113] The Church, by contrast, now advocates *quince años* celebrations for boys, which have been celebrated in the Dioceses of Fort Worth and San Angelo, Texas.[114] And Erevia attempts to claim the reception as a continuation of the religious celebration: "The fiesta, following the Mass, is an important part of the celebration. It is an expression of gratitude to God for the lives of the young people."[115]

While the Church and society engage in this power struggle as "spiritual benefactors," Hispanic girls and their families all over the United States are celebrating *quinceañeras* under the influence of both institutions. As a result, many of the girls are confused. In San Antonio in 1998, I surveyed 144 Catholic high school girls between the ages of fourteen and nineteen, 79 percent of whom stated on informal questionaires that their backgrounds were at least partly Mexican or Mexican-American.[116] I expected this sample of predominantly Latino-American teenaged girls, who talked of either attending or "standing in the courts [at]" *quinceañeras* almost weekly, and whose families valued Catholic education, to be well informed regarding the *quiceañera* and its sacred meaning. Indeed, 77 percent had attended at least one *quiceañera*, debut, or Sweet Sixteen,[117] revealing the popularity of these celebrations, and thirteen girls specifically had celebrated or planned to celebrate *quinceañeras*. But a closer look at the girls' responses demonstrates their superficial understanding even of the terminology involved. In particular, one, girl who had celebrated her *quinceañera* wrote that she did not know whether or not she had had a debut. Two had celebrated or planned to celebrate debuts and Sweet Sixteens (implying a combination of the two, since planning and financing two celebrations of this magnitude for one girl is unheard of). Three thought they had celebrated or planned to celebrate a *quinceañera*, a debut, and a Sweet Sixteen (a literal impossibility, since combining a *quince años* celebration with a Sweet Sixteen is anachronous). Eight girls said they had celebrated or planned to celebrate Sweet Sixteens, one of whom believed she had taken classes for it at a church. And eleven said they had celebrated or planned to celebrate debuts and *quinceañeras*, four of whom said they had taken classes for them at churches. Having been bombarded throughout their lives by conflicting messages about the *quinceañera*, many of these past and prospective *quinceañeras*, conceivably the teens best informed about the tradition, revealed either bafflement or (like Salcedo and many others who use the terms *debut* and *quinceañera* interchangeably) an understanding more secular than sacred regarding celebration.

Moreover, Church-sponsored *quinceañera* preparation programs do not necessarily override the messages these girls receive from their other "spiritual benefactor," American popular culture. Overall, 36 of the girls surveyed—25 percent—either had celebrated or planned to celebrate one of the three customs, and seven of them had taken classes for it at a church. Clearly, these seven girls had prepared for the *quinceañera*; the Church specifically offers *quinceañera* preparation programs to educate prospective *quinceañeras* and their families about this rite of passage. But five of the seven girls who had taken Church-sponsored classes called their celebrations something other than *quinceañeras*—either debuts or Sweet Sixteens. Thus, even after participating in Church-sponsored *quinceañera* preparation programs, over 70 percent of these seven girls referred to their *quinceañeras* by names that American culture has popularized. Similarly, while 55 of all the girls knew that a *quinceañera* is a party to celebrate a girl's transition into womanhood, and 48 called it a girl's fifteenth birthday party, in their definitions of the *quinceañera*, only 10 mentioned God, baptismal promises, the Church, Mass, or the Virgin Mary. In fact, 13 girls defined the *quinceañera* solely as a coming-out party or a girl's introduction into society.

REVIEW OF THE "BEQUESTS" AND A PROPOSAL FOR A NEW LEGACY

On the whole, as "spiritual benefactor," America alters the faith of its immigrants and their descendents—its "spiritual beneficiaries"—as they assimilate into the culture of the United States. Through Latinos' integration into the dominant culture in particular, American popular culture has changed the *quinceañera* tradition and continues to do so. In this case, the Church and American popular culture share the role of "spiritual benefactor" and even compete for it. American popular culture has commercialized the *quinceañera*; made it resemble a traditional American wedding; cultivated the attitude that an expensive reception is the most important element of the custom; and fused the *quinceañera* with other traditions, specifically the debut and Sweet Sixteen. The Catholic Church in America has likewise redefined the *quinceañera*, tending to ascribe the custom primarily to communal aspects of ancient fertility rites that stressed divinities and religious beliefs (instead of recognizing the almost completely sexual nature of these indigenous rites, or acknowledging other conspicuous sources that emphasized a young woman's readiness for marriage, or conceding that the *quinceañera*'s precise origin is, in fact, unknown), and reshaped the tradition to bring it in line with Catholic teachings. And even though the

Church's *quinceañera* preparation programs are increasingly common, they do not always outweigh the powerful messages Latino Americans receive from American popular culture. Latino Americans express mixed feeling about the Church's changes to the *quinceañera*, and many Hispanic teenaged girls, who are most affected by these changes, are embroiled by the conflicting messages they receive from the disparate facets of their American culture.

To help remedy this situation, I suggest that—if they have not done so already—priests of Hispanic parishioners establish and educate lay teams to lead well-defined *quinceañera* ministries at their parishes, ministries that engage families in dialogue, beginning at the early stages of their *quinceañera* planning and preparation (before they have placed a deposit on a hotel ballroom). At least three questions should take precedence in this dialogue. First, What is the *quinceañera*? The answer to this question could address the truth about *quinceañera* history. Being certified to teach secondary students and having recently instructed Catholic school girls in this age group myself, I see less potential harm in the Church's teaching today's fifteen-year-old girls what little is known about the *quinceañera*'s origins, than in censoring half of it and editing the rest. An honest presentation of the facts could naturally lead into a discussion of the second question: What does it mean to celebrate the *quinceañera* in the Church? Theoretically, Church-sponsored *quinceañera* preparation programs already address this issue, but my students' responses indicate that, at least at their parishes in San Antonio, the concept needs to be taught more thoroughly (or more competently, or both), perhaps over several months or more, with weekly meetings, like the R.C.I.A. (Rite for the Christian Initiation of Adults). If this seems excessive, compare it to the amount of time these girls and their families spend perceiving the messages of American popular culture as they plan their *quinceañeras*. Whether or not the Church continues to reshape the *quinceañera*, the wedding and *quinceañera* industries and the media will.

The third question confronts this problem: How does the media influence a girl's (and her family's) choices about her *quinceañera*? Prospective *quinceañeras* and their families need to think critically about the media's power over the decisions they make so as not to remain "passive recipients"[118] of American popular culture's "bequests." Less affluent families may need to be empowered to evaluate the media's messages and consider alternatives to extravagant receptions, even for the sake of the girls they plan to honor. It does not profit a young woman when her family runs into debt from celebrating her *quinceañera* and then cannot afford its rent or to help finance her education or wedding a few years later. In the United States and in Mexico, the current trend is to allow the girl to choose whether to celebrate a traditional *quinceañera* at all, or to travel abroad or receive a large sum of money or a car instead. From a practical viewpoint, working-class Latino-American families would be well advised to ask themselves: Why not hold a simple *quinceañera* celebration and two or three years later, possess the financial resources to send this young woman to college, where she can develop the skills that are increasingly necessary to become self-sufficient in this country?

Protestant ministers may also wish to consider developing *quinceañera* ministries because about one-third of America's Hispanics are not Catholic, but

Protestant and evangelical.[119] If Protestant churches are celebrating *quinceañeras* (my research does not indicate so), they may wish to consult with one another and with Catholic priests who have established successful *quinceañera* ministries at their parishes. For the result of some Hispanics changing their church membership from Catholic to Protestant "has not been a competition, but rather an ecumenical effort by Catholics, Pentecostals, and other Protestants to come together in a respectful effort to figure out how best to serve Latino Christians."[120]

In the final analysis, the epigraph that precedes this essay demonstrates the power of American popular culture as a "spiritual benefactor" (though a mainly negative one) and its ongoing commercialization of the *quinceañera*. The only American institution that has significantly counteracted this influence has been another "spiritual benefactor," the American Catholic Church. Although, at least in some cases, the Church has taken considerable liberties in constructing a history of the *quinceañera* and reshaped the custom from its almost purely social context, it apparently has done so as a means of justifying its own continued celebrations of the *quinceañera* Mass and as a tool for catechizing the *quinceañeras* and their families. It remains to be seen which "spiritual bequest" will outweigh the other for future *quinceañeras*. Will the girls allow themselves to be subjected to American popular culture, or will they follow the path taken by Araceli Gallegos, one of four *quinceañeras* who prepared for a joint celebration of the rite at Sacred Heart Parish in San Jose? According to this young Latina, ". . . now we need to change those [*quinceañera*] traditions and see that what is important is to give thanks to God."[121]

NOTES

1. Denise Van Patten, *2001 Dolls: New Barbie® Doll Releases* (2001), http://www.collectdolls.about.com/hobbies/collectdolls/library/idex/blidex78.htm (16 June 2001).

2. This term is pronounced "KEEN-se-an-YEH-ra," according to Donatella Lorch, "*Quinceañera*: A Girl Grows Up," *New York Times*, 1 February 1996: C1. For consistency throughout this article, foreign words are italicized, whether or not they are italicized in their sources.

3. Michele Salcedo, *Quinceañera! The Essential Guide to Planning the Perfect Sweet Fifteen Celebration* (New York: Henry Holt and Company, 1997), 4.

4. Greg Dues, *Catholic Customs and Traditions: A Popular Guide* (Mystic, Conn: Twenty-Third Publications, 1989), 173.

5. Erich S. Gruen, "Cultural Fictions and Cultural Identity," *Transactions of the American Philological Association* 123 (1993): 3.

6. Gruen, "Cultural Fictions," 3.

7. Jay P. Dolan and Gilberto M. Hinojosa, eds., *Mexican Americans and the Catholic Church 1900–1965*, Vol. 1 of *The Notre Dame History of Hispanic Catholics in the U.S.* (Notre Dame, Ind.: University of Notre Dame Press, 1994), 33, 92.

8. Dolan and Hinojosa, *Mexican Americans*, 13.

9. Interdicasterial Commission for the *Catechism of the Catholic Church*, *Catechism of the Catholic Church*, trans. United States Catholic Conference, Inc. (Cittia del Vaticano: Libreria Editrice Vaticana, 1994), 415.

10. Dolan and Hinojosa, *Mexican Americans*, 178. Beatrice Griffith describes an *altarcito*: "There stands a statue of the Virgin (before a votive candle) adorned with fresh or paper flowers. Important letters, birth or marriage certificates, are frequently placed

on the little shelf, together with the rosary, crucifix, special medals, novena prayers, and probably a small picture of the Virgin of Guadalupe."

11. Dolan and Hinojosa, *Mexican Americans*, 178.

12. Ibid., 179.

13. Ibid., 191.

14. Ibid.

15. Ibid., 178–79.

16. Ibid., 179.

17. Salcedo, *Quinceañera!*, 14.

18. Norma E. Cantú, "*La Quinceañera*: Towards an Ethnographic Analysis of a Life-Cycle Ritual," *Southern Folklore* 1 (1999): 73.

19. Susan Orlean, "Old-fashioned Girls," *New Yorker* (12 February 1990): 82.

20. Ibid.

21. Dale Hoyt Palfrey, "*La Quinceañera*: An Hispanic Celebration of Budding Womanhood," *Mexico Connect*, 1996–97, http://www.mexconnect,com/mex_/travel/dpalfreydpquince.html (2 May 1999).

22. Ruth Horowitz, "The Power of Ritual in a Chicano Community: A Young Woman's Status and Expanding Family Ties," *Marriage and Family Review* 19 (1993): 267.

23. Salcedo, *Quinceañera!*, 89–90.

24. Valentina Napolitano, "Becoming a *Mujercita*: Rituals, Fiestas, and Religious Discourses," *Journal of the Royal Anthropological Institute* 3 (1997): 282.

25. Cantú, "*La Quinceañera*," 73–74.

26. Napolitano, "Becoming a *Mujercita*," 281.

27. Cantú, "*La Quinceañera*," 75.

28. Elly Moran, interview by the author, San Antonio, Texas, 12 May 1999.

29. Ibid.

30. Ibid.

31. Cantú, "*La Quinceañera*," 76–77.

32. Salcedo, *Quinceañera!*, 36, 7.

33. Ibid., 6, 9.

34. Mark J. Brummel, C.M.F., ed., "*Tienes 15 Años* (Now That You Are 15)," *El Momento Católico* (Chicago: Claretian Publications, 1993), 4.

35. Ibid.

36. Ibid., 5.

37. Ibid., 6.

38. Angela Erevia, M.C.D.P., *Quince Años: Celebrating a Tradition: A Handbook for Parish Teams* (San Antonio, Texas: Missionary Catechists of Divine Providence, 1996), 15.

39. Ibid., 16–17.

40. Cantú, "*La Quinceañera*," 74.

41. Erevia's comparison mentions sexuality as a "sacred area" that indigenous adolescents were taught to "appreciate" and states that these girls "were considered sacred, because by the gift of sex, they were blessed with the power to share human life by creating other human beings." This is practically identical to her explanation of the Christian tradition's teaching regarding sexuality. She also states that the indigenous young people "had to perform certain duties for the community," but does not confess the strikingly sexual nature of these duties. Erevia, *Quince Años*, 17.

42. Rosa María Icaza, C.C.V.I., "*Quinceañera* Celebration," The Mini Pastoral Program, Mexican American Cultural Center, The National Catholic Institute for Pastoral Education and Language Studies, San Antonio, Texas. June 1996. Lecture.

43. Moran, interview.

44. Salcedo, *Quinceañera!*, 9.

45. Moran, interview.

46. Salcedo, *Quinceañera!*, 35.

47. Quoted in Orlean, "Old-fashioned Girls," 86.

48. Orlean, "Old-fashioned Girls," 82.

49. Ibid.

50. Monica Humbard, "Minority Marketing Equals Major Sales Opportunities: Expand Your Sales Base by Reaching Out to Ethnic Customers," *Floral Retailing* 5 (2000), http://floralretailing.com/MayArticle5.html (17 June 2001).

51. Orlean, "Old-fashioned Girls," 82.

52. Salcedo, *Quinceañera!*, 175, 21, 18.

53. Ibid., 28.

54. Ibid., 79.

55. Ibid., 27.

56. Ibid., 70.

57. Ibid., 75.

58. Ibid., 180.

59. Lorch, "*Quinceañera*," C1.

60. Salcedo, *Quinceañera!*, 15.

61. Monica Ortega, "Special Traditions for Your *Quinceañera*," *Latina Bride* (16 September 1997), www.latinabride.com/engquince.html (2 May 1999).

62. Quoted in Salcedo, *Quinceañera!*, 50.

63. Salcedo, *Quinceañera!*, 38.

64. Horowitz, "The Power of Ritual," 267.

65. Salcedo, *Quinceañera!*, 45.

66. Ibid., 38.

67. Horowitz, "The Power of Ritual," 258.

68. Ibid., 270.

69. Salcedo, *Quinceañera!*, 15.

70. Ibid., 183.

71. Horwitz, "The Power of Ritual," 270.

72. Salcedo, *Quinceañera!*, 16.

73. Ortega, "Special Traditions," 1.

74. Salcedo, *Quinceañera!*, 16.

75. Ibid., 14, 6.

76. Ibid., 54, 71.

77. Ortega, "Special Traditions," 1.

78. "Your *Quince Años* Are Coming: Counting Down to the Big Day," *Latina Bride* (16 September 1997), http://www.latinabride.com/engquincecalendar.html (2 May 1999).

79. *Quince Años*, Angela Erevia, M.C.D.P., narr. and project dir., Gerardo L. Rueda, dir. of photography and line prod./ed., Alan Medrano, prod. San Antonio: Missionary Catechists of Providence, 1996. Videocassette.

80. Cantú, "*La Quinceañera*," 74.

81. Horowitz, "The Power of Ritual," 260.

82. Moran, interview.

83. Palfrey, "*La Quinceañera*," 1–2.

84. Salcedo, *Quinceañera!*, 25.

85. Ibid., 79.

86. Ibid., 222.

87. Lorch, "*Quinceañera*," C4.

88. Horowitz, "The Power of Ritual," 263.

89. Lorch, "*Quinceañera*," C1, C4.

90. Salcedo, *Quinceañera!*, 7.

91. Orlean, "Old-fashioned Girls," 82–83.

92. Salcedo, *Quinceañera!*, 7.

93. Ibid.

94. Ibid., 36.

95. Quoted in Lorch, "*Quinceañera*," C4.

96. Lorch "*Quinceañera*," C4.

97. Quoted in Salcedo, *Quinceañera!*, 41.

98. Quoted in Lorch, "*Quinceañera*," C4.

99. Orlean, "Old-fashioned Girls," 83.

100. "The *Quinceañera*," *Our Family*, Patti Elizondo, host, J. Robert Gutierrez and Lina Del Roble, narrs., Carlos Amezcua, prod., Pablo San Martin, Jr. and Carlos R. Sanchez, eds., San Antonio Catholic Television of San Antonio, CTSA, 3 May 2000. Television program.

101. "The *Quinceañera*."

102. "The *Quinceañera*."

103. Orlean, "Old-fashioned Girls," 84.

104. Horowitz, "The Power of Ritual," 259.

105. Ibid., 275.

106. Orlean, "Old-fashioned Girls," 84.

107. Quoted in Orlean, "Old-fashioned Girls," 85.

108. Orlean, "Old-fashioned Girls," 88.

109. Horowitz, "The Power of Ritual," 270.

110. Salcedo, *Quinceañera!*, 221.

111. Ibid., 221–22.

112. Orlean, "Old-fashioned Girls," 85.

113. Ibid., 88.

114. Salcedo, *Quinceañera!*, 220.

115. Erevia, *Quince Años*, 37.

116. This percentage is conservative. In one school, 46 out of 49 girls who completed the questionnaire claimed a Mexican or Mexican-American background. The other three chose not to answer the question, though one of them, who had recently immigrated from Mexico, completed the rest of the questionnaire in Spanish. In the other school, some girls with Spanish surnames and whose parents spoke Spanish but not English wrote that their backgrounds were not Mexican or Mexican-American.

117. Again, this percentage is conservative, as several other girls either did not know how many they had attended or did not answer the question. But all of those girls' answers to the open-ended questions revealed that they knew what went on at the celebrations.

118. Gruen, "Cultural Fictions," 3.

119. Joseph Claude Harris, "Are American Catholics in Decline?," *America* 20 (2000): 13.

120. James Blair, "New Christian Culture Emerges as Churches Appeal to Latinos," *Christian Science Monitor* 192 (1997): 5.

121. Quoted in "The *Quinceañera*."

Becoming a Mujercita
Rituals, Fiestas, and Religious Discourses

Valentina Napolitano

INTRODUCTION

There have been few published studies of the celebration of girls' fifteenth birthdays in Mexico, especially among urban, non-indigenous populations (Cardenas 1987). Recent literature on gender in urban Mexico and Latin America has focused more on class, ethnicity (e.g., Arizpe 1977; Beneria & Roldan 1987; Nash & Safa 1976; 1986) and women's participation in social movements (e.g., Alvarez 1990; Logan 1988; Westwood & Radcliffe 1993), than on the study of rites of passage (Lomnitz & Perez-Lizuar 1987) and life cycles. These latter themes were once developed in Latin American ethnography by scholars working within the Culture and Personality approach (e.g., Díaz 1966; Díaz-Guerrero 1975; Fromm & Maccoby 1970; Kemper 1977; Romanucci-Ross 1973), which later scholars rightly criticized for employing ethnocentric psychological paradigms and a non-historical, essentialist view of the self.

Studies of women's participation in social movements in Latin America have questioned essentialist views of women, deconstructed aspects of motherhood, elaborated on the role of the state in gender discourse and argued for a continuity between public and private spheres (Craske 1993; Westwood & Radcliffe 1993). Moreover, recent theoretical work on gender identity has developed a focus on the embodiment of gender experience and on the multiplicity of gendered subjectivity (Moore 1994) and has examined the negotiation of gender attributes in specific Mexican and Latin American cases (Gutmann 1996; Wade 1994). This work is of considerable importance in the study of female rituals and life-cycles as it opens up issues concerning the reversibility of gender acquisitions and therefore the non-linearity of life-rituals. It has also contributed to an awareness that metaphors of status completion—often used by anthropologists to analyse initiation rituals—hinge on a particular notion of personhood (Strathern 1993).

Valentina Napolitano: "Becoming a *Mujercita*," first published in *Across the Boundaries of Belief: Contemporary Issues in the Anthropology of Religion*, edited by Morton Klass and Maxine Weisgrau. Boulder: Westview Press, 1999.

In this article I discuss the celebration of girls' fifteenth birthdays and show why this ritual has become important in the process of creation of female identity in a Mexican low-income neighborhood. Both the *fiesta* and Mass, which together constitute the ritual, embody a process of female self-becoming involving both continuities and discontinuities (Crapanzano 1992: 262), as well as a public recognition of a girl's and her family's social empowerment.

The motivations for celebrating these rituals, and indeed for not celebrating them, are important for understanding their meaning. I will present several case histories to show how decisions about whether or not to celebrate a feast for a girl's fifteenth birthday—and on what scale—depend on a family's religious beliefs, on its respectability in the neighborhood, on its attitudes to girls' education, and on the negotiation of female attributes between clerical and lay agents and within and between families.

The clerical agents who figure in this study are mainly part of the "new" Catholic Church—or, as it is called, the Church of the *Comunidades Eclesiales de Base* (CEBs), or "Christian Base Communities."[1] This Catholic discourse challenges existing values attached to "traditional" rituals as far as the balance between religious celebration and popular *fiestas* is concerned. Priests have introduced a collective Mass instead of an individual one to celebrate the girls' birthdays and have criticized large-scale expenditure on *fiestas* as aspects of consumerism and family "protagonism" (that is, status-seeking). CEBs discourse has been considered a progressive "route to democratization" in Latin America, enabling people to see themselves as active "voices" in the process of change (Alvarez 1990; Levine 1992: 29), even if in some cases it may still be used by the Church hierarchy to convey "traditional" values of hierarchical control (Levine 1985: 310). However, CEBs discourse has also been questioned—both by analysts and CEBs members—concerning whether it really challenges gender hierarchies and advances the raising of female consciousness, or instead subordinates women's issues to problems of economic injustice and oppression (Alvarez 1990; Drogus 1990: 66; Hewitt 1991: 64). In fact, the recent decline of participation in CEBs in Latin America, in favor of Evangelical and Protestant movements, is also due to CEBs' difficulties in addressing issues of gender and race diversity and thus erasing internal differentiations among the poor (Burdick 1992: 183).

I analyse the ritual of the fifteenth birthday at three different levels: in terms of the form and content it assumes in CEBs discourse; through the exegesis of the religious and sexual symbolism connected with the celebration as part of a process of gender and family identity; and finally, through a more detailed contextual analysis of this exegesis by means of case-studies. Such analysis reveals that the symbolism of the ritual is not fixed. Rather, different aspects of its symbolic potential are stressed depending on a girl's family circumstances and the participants' negotiation of constructs of gender identity.

THE SETTING

This study was carried out in the *colonia popular*[2] of Lomas de Polanco in the south of Guadalajara (the second largest Mexican city). This neighborhood has an estimated population of 30,000—the majority being employed as factory workers, construction workers, and street vendors. Since the early sixties it has been peopled by migrant settlers from the regions of Jalisco, Zacatecas and Michoacÿn.[3] It is a famous neighborhood in the history of Guadalajara due to a remarkable social mobilization—inspired by the intervention of Jesuits (Morfin Otero 1979; Sanchez 1979)—which took place from the mid-1970s until the late 1980s and led, after a long confrontation with the municipal authorities, to free installation of a sewage system and other basic services. The Jesuits developed a strong network of CEBs, inspired by liberation theology; however, since the beginning of the 1990s, people's participation in this movement has decreased due to a combination of factors. Basic services have been installed and economic stratification has increased. Consequently, the language of "fighting for basic services" and of "the communality of being poor" has had less resonance than it had in the 1970s and 1980s (Napolitano 1995: 56): once the movement's demands were met, it tended to lose its reason for existing (Foweraker 1995: 105).[4]

There are two parishes in the neighborhood. Padre Nemo has been in charge of the parish of the Anunciación since 1989, and has been very keen to renew the work of the CEBs. Padres Rodolfo and Jorge have had responsibility for the bigger parish of the Santa Magdalena. They support the CEBs, but are much less radical than the Jesuits and Padre Nemo.

THE ESTABLISHMENT OF THE FIFTEENTH BIRTHDAY CELEBRATION

The custom of celebrating a girl's fifteenth birthday is widespread in Mexican society. It consists of a Mass celebrated to give "gracias a Dios" (thanks to God), followed by a *fiesta*. The size of the party varies according to the means of the family and the godparents. This celebration was originally a feast celebrated in upper and upper-middle class strata but it has now filtered down to lower sectors of the population. In certain contexts in Lomas de Polanco, the decision not to celebrate the feast while having the means to do so or, conversely, the inability to celebrate it for economic reasons, can be read as signs of high or low family status.

The origins of the feast are unknown to people in Lomas de Polanco. Old women do not recollect it in their accounts of the past. Middle-aged women remember that rich families in their villages of origin did celebrate the feast, but it was a custom only of the "gente de dinero" (rich people). Some women younger than forty and brought up in the city have celebrated it, but here the celebration constituted a small family gathering without a real *fiesta* afterwards, and no special dress was bought or made for the occasion.[5] In recent years, the celebration has gone out of fashion among the upper and upper-middle classes in Guadalajara. Girls prefer to celebrate their birthdays either at a disco or with a trip abroad, as is the case in Mexico City (Lomnitz & Perez-Lizuar 1987: 166–67). The fifteenth birthday was originally celebrated as a ball—a girl's presentation to high society. The symbolism used in the feast recalled, and still recalls, elements of European culture (for instance, waltzes, performances of classical music, maids of honor and pages).

The first reports of the feast started to appear in the *Sociales* (social events) section of Guadalajara newspapers during the early 1940s. There are no church records, since the ritual is not a sacrament. The *fiesta* was celebrated in the house, and was an occasion for making family connections manifest. It reinforced family status and social cohesion among a specific social class. Nowadays, press reports still present an "ideal" model of the celebration of the fifteenth birthday, a standard unattainable by the population of Lomas de Polanco but still deferred to by *quinceañeras* (girls fifteen years old) and their families.

These ideals are obviously acquired through the mass media, especially soap operas. Soap operas are a primary means through which images of upper-class life style and consumption patterns become familiar to low-income populations, and middle-class values are transformed into hegemonic ones. This is reflected, for instance, in the choice of the girl's dress or the ritual paraphernalia for the feast celebration, as I discuss below.

In the catechism of this ritual, priests supporting the CEBs are critical of these forms of modernization, consumption, and "protagonism." In the catechism class, which takes place in the parish of the Santa Magdalena a few days before the celebration, some of these issues are discussed. Other themes touched upon include the physical and psychological changes which the girls are undergoing and the different ways at their disposal for becoming active agents in the community Church. The *quinceañeras* are taught by Nubia, a female catechist, that a similar feast was celebrated in the time of the Toltecs and the Aztec warriors. Girls who undertook the celebration were ready to be chosen by a male of the tribe and taken to the mountain. Soon after, they become pregnant for the sake of "community" reproduction. References are also made to similar feasts celebrated at the beginning of this century in Jewish communities, and to the balls intended to introduce girls into society among the middle-European upper class in the last century. In this allusive way the subject of sexuality is introduced to the catechism class, and continuity with the past is related to a "natural" female sexual status. However, that continuity is not traced via the girl's own mother or grandmother. The catechist, and some *quinceañeras*, are aware that senior female relatives have not celebrated this feast. Nonetheless the celebration of the fifteenth birthday becomes a connection with the "ancestors," a link with the past acted out in the present.

THE CELEBRATION: A WEDDING WITHOUT A HUSBAND

The ritual of the fifteenth birthday involves girls learning about gender identity and the construction of the female body. It does not correspond exactly to van Gennep's (1977) concept of a rite of passage, nor is it a process whose fluidity is counterposed to a static social structure (Turner 1974). While it is constituted by moments of separation, liminality, and reincorporation in the stages of the Mass and the *fiesta*, the ritual is not obligatory. Girls in Lomas de Polanco acquire the status of "being a woman" with or without celebrating it. Rather, the ritual indicates ways in which a girl's image is constructed by the actors involved; it also affects the girl's own self-perception, and enables certain forms of social control over the female body.

The rite of passage starts with the Mass. The girl arrives at the church accompanied by her parents. She wears a ball dress, preferably pink or peach colored. White is not a fashionable color, probably because it is the color of "real" weddings (this rite resembles a wedding, as I discuss below). The ideal style of the dress is "nineteenth century," with big round skirts, voile, embroideries, and high heeled shoes. However, many families in Lomas de Polanco cannot afford this type of dress and so girls choose cheaper versions, often home-made by close relatives; dresses are seldom bought in the specialized shops in the city center. The girl is often carefully coiffured with various trinkets such as small artificial flowers.

The girl, her parents, godparents, and *chambelano* (male chaperon) wait for the priest to come to the entrance of the church. Then the girl, on her godfather's arm, walks in a procession towards the altar, following the priest. The *chambelano* walks and sits just behind her. "Tradition" demands that the girl be surrounded by seven *damas* (ladies) and seven *chambelanos*, all dressed in the same way, but this is hardly ever the case in Lomas de Polanco celebrations, though whenever possible there is at least one *chambelano*.[6] The girl is led by her close relatives towards the altar, and is then left alone to receive the Mass. The celebration of the Mass can be interpreted as a liminal stage, in which she is recognized as a newly born *mujercita* (little woman) both in the eyes of God and those close to her. When the Mass is over, the *quinceañera* leaves her bouquets of fresh flowers for the Virgin behind the altar. While the girl entered the church with her godparents, she leaves the church arm-in-arm with her *chambelano*. The *quinceañera* may have a secret boyfriend before her fifteenth birthday. If this is the case, the *chambelano* is preferably not the same person; normally he is a friend of a similar age, ideally a few years older, but never younger than she is.

Being "handed over" to the *chambelano* constitutes the first stage of her reincorporation. The *chambelano*'s behavior towards the girl is very different from his behavior towards her in everyday life. He wears a suit and tie; he is very gentle to the *quinceañera* and often arrives with flowers for her—acts which in another public context, at that age, might be interpreted as showing lack of masculinity. Like the separation, the reincorporation takes place by means of a "protecting" male figure, whose role is to defend the girl from unfamiliar, male, sources of sexual attraction.

This phase of the ritual parallels the "handing over" of the groom to his bride during the wedding celebration (which itself ends the period in a girl's life initiated by the fifteenth birthday celebration). This "handing over" is symbolized by the *muertito*. The *muertito* is a little drama which takes place in some wedding *fiestas* in Lomas de Polanco: the groom is taken away by his male friends, stripped of some of his clothes and then given back to the bride who has to help him dress again. It portrays how marriage should end the self-indulgence typical of a bachelor lifestyle, and makes the groom "subject" to the exclusive care of his bride.

Most of the fifteenth birthday fiestas that I witnessed in Lomas de Polanco took place at home. Food is given to the guests after the opening dances, with the godparents served first. Young guests come to the party especially to dance and drink. The *quinceañera* dances to the opening music, first with her godfather and then with her father or her maternal uncle if her father is absent. An important episode of the ritual is a special dance with the *chambelano* and, if present, the *damas*.

The *quinceañera* often choreographs a waltz routine with her *chambelano*. Some girls rehearse for as much as three months to learn the steps and to acquire enough confidence to perform in front of a large number of friends and relatives. In her dance the *quinceañera* often directs the movements of the *chambelano*, thus leading him on a public occasion. When asked why they dance a waltz, *quinceañeras* reply that it is somehow elegant: a *quinceañera* without a waltz is not a real *quinceañera*. Indeed, if the music was not a waltz there would be no difference between a *quinceañera* celebration and any other *fiesta*.

This dance is a powerful emotional experience. The girl is in the public eye and fear of "failing" and appearing clumsy is a recurrent concern:

> I was very nervous about the waltz coming out fine. I was afraid of forgetting the steps, of getting embarrassed in front of many people, but never in my life will I forget that moment (Nubia, catechist).

This dance, often interpreted by the clergy as a mere form without content (see below), is for the *quinceañera* an experience of a new ability to perform in public, and of the emotions connected with a change in self-identity. The girl's tensions usually fade as the dance goes on and she, with her *chambelano*, assumes more self-confidence. As the *fiesta* develops, her parents and older brothers check that potential drunks are kept under control. The celebration generally ends around midnight.[7] It is clear that the excitement, the nervousness, and the sense of fulfilment that the *fiesta* and the ball generate are powerful bodily and emotional experiences for the girls. In the words of one *quinceañera*:

> I felt realized, and it is better than the wedding celebration because you are innocent about many things, whereas now I see all the good and bad. . . . At the fifteenth birthday celebration, you are more fulfilled because you do not see what awaits you.

CEBS DISCOURSE: CHANGING FORM AND CONTENT OF TRADITIONAL RITUALS

Anthropological readings of ritual as a means of maintaining social control and cohesion are very similar to CEBs' attitudes towards celebrations of "traditional" rituals. To a certain extent, CEBs' understanding of religious rituals and popular celebrations is distinct from more orthodox Catholic interpretations. And CEBs discourse can only be fully understood if it is studied in a complex religious arena including different and often conflicting voices among the grassroots and the leaders of the CEBs themselves (Burdick 1994: 196).

The CEBs' goal is to "use the symbols of popular religion and give them a new interpretation of their real meaning" (Padre Nemo). In other words, the parishes' political wish is to fill "traditional" and long-established rituals with "new and truthful contents." This has happened, for instance, in celebrations of the Virgin of Guadalupe, when in sermons and social drama the Virgin becomes an "Amazon" aiding the efforts of enslaved people in the process of liberation, rather than a passive listener and consoler of human sadness as she is portrayed in the images of the "traditional" Church.[8] The Virgin is a polysemic symbol in Mexico, whose imagery can stand both for sufferings which give strength and legitimacy to women (Melhuus 1992: 159) and for the redemption of the community, since the power of giving birth and caring for children can be seen as balancing out male political self-interest and corruption (Martin 1990: 486).

Thus, the metaphor of fighting for social justice, which the CEBs have introduced, imports a "new" sense of resistance into a "traditional" symbol. Moreover, the *fiestas* promoted by the *Comunidades* focus on the communal gathering rather than on the diversions, the food and the music: the Mass should evangelize on social and political injustice, and expenditure on entertainments should be kept down. But some believers oppose such changes since the celebrations lose the ambience they used to have in the village or on the ranch. Consequently, the dismissal of "traditional" devices typical of village *fiestas*, and the introduction of "new"—socially and politically oriented—contents in the celebration of the Mass by some clerical agents challenge the "traditional" Catholic division between the mundane, the political, and the religious, and raise questions about what a "traditional" celebration is, and who controls it.

The celebration of the fifteenth birthday in Lomas de Polanco also raises issues about the "new" contents of "traditional" rituals. Since the fifteenth birthday celebration is not one of the seven Catholic sacraments, and is a relatively new ritual, the interpretation of it is an open field both for clerical and pastoral agents. Catholic teaching stresses girls' "closeness to nature"; the purity of their bodies at the Mass should cause them to honor God for their having arrived "intact" at this point in life. The Mass also stresses the duty to "take a right path" and become part of the community by participating in activities such as children's catechism, youth theatre, choirs, and *Comunidades*.[9] Failure to participate in such community activities is interpreted as a lack of maturity and an inability to accept the responsibility appropriate to a mature Catholic person. Since the arrival of Padre Nemo and Padre Rodolfo, the celebration in Lomas de Polanco has taken place in groups, but tensions between family and community loyalties have arisen in relation to this communal celebration. Some families have accordingly decided to celebrate the Mass in parishes outside Lomas de Polanco.

In the Santa Magdalena, all the *quinceañeras* who have their birthday in the same month go to Mass on the last Saturday of that month. Padre Rodolfo and Padre Jorge, in their sermons, underline that this Mass reaffirms the principle of the baptism as a renewed initiation into the life of the Catholic Church.[10] A former priest in the Santa Magdalena, Padre Hermilio, points out the problem the Church faces in understanding and interpreting a "new" ritual which acquires importance in people's lives. However he, like the other priests in Lomas de Polanco, emphasizes a search for "meaning," stressing the "word" above the "act."

> There is also—and we must not forget it—a mentality which is not easy to change. It looks for the celebration without catechism, *the act without words.* . . . The major-

ity of the people want the Mass as a step in order to celebrate the "fiesta", which is sometimes reduced to an expression of consumerism and of a materialist society (Cardenas Gonzalez 1987: 122; my translation and emphasis).

The polarization between a meaningful act and a *"fiesta* in itself" is drawn in the catechism used by the *Comunidades*. Padres Rodolfo, Nemo, and Hermilio believe that the Mass for the fifteenth birthday entails a transformation of girls' consciousness and focus of action from familial and personal to communal levels. Padre Nemo and Padre Rodolfo affirm that people need to overcome the individualistic and egoistic tendencies which create "protagonism." This celebration—to them—becomes an opportunity for strengthening a sense of community rather than an occasion for family status differentiation. "Protagonism," in the words of the priests, is associated with individualism, urban atomization, and materialist culture.

The "resistance" of a part of the population to a communal celebration suggests that additional issues are at stake. Priests and their associates underestimate the importance of the Mass and the *fiesta* as *experiences* in the process of the creation of female self-identity. The fifteenth birthday celebration is "the day" of the girl: in fact, the priest has to address each girl by her name; otherwise "if the priests do not call her by name, it is not her Mass" (Padre Hermilio). This reflects the fact that a girl's name is very rarely used in speaking about her. A girl is "the daughter of the woman who sells chickens . . . the daughter of those who sell tacos . . . the daughter of my godfather" and so on, usages which, to a certain extent, imply that she is not recognized as a full social person.

The celebration of this feast also highlights a tension between a young woman's desire for freedom, and the "respectability" which her family maintains through its control over her. On the one hand, the girl is the center of the feast and expects subsequently to receive more freedom of action and decision-making within the close family environment. However, this freedom is rarely granted, and family control actually becomes greater. The *fiestas*, being a form of differentiation of family status, constitute an important moment for a girl's self-identity and for the identity and reputation of her family. Through CEBs' evangelization people may become "aware" that *fiestas* can entail "unnecessary" financial commitments; nonetheless many spend considerable amounts, regardless of these criticisms.

BECOMING A *MUJERCITA*: THE TIME OF ILLUSION

I shall now analyse the symbolism of the fifteenth birthday celebration in the light of several case-histories.

In common language, the fifteenth year is referred to as the most glorious for a girl. Expressions such as *parece de quince* ("you look very well"; literally, "you look like a fifteen-year-old"), to *pusieron como una de quince* (literally, "they made you like a fifteen-year-old," meaning that the person has recovered completely from some illness) identify this age with physical health and vigor. In the imagery of both young and older women in Lomas de Polanco, the fifteenth year represents a period of illusion, *la ilusión de los quince*:

You are like blossoming flowers . . . what will shine is not your dress, but your soul, the purity of your soul . . . now you can really start to be somebody (Nubia).

The time of illusion in female life is that period when girls hope to enjoy themselves before assuming responsibility for their own families. The expression is used by women of various ages, but it can also be used by fathers to refer to their daughters. This period continues throughout the engagement, and revolves around a "fantasy" concerning life and, especially, love. The fifteenth birthday celebration coincides with the acknowledgment by the family (especially the father) that a daughter is ready to have a sweetheart (if she does not have one already). The father gives her the *permiso de porta* (literally, the licence of the door), the authorization to see her boyfriend on the threshold of the house for a set period during the evening. The times and modalities of this licence depend on the strictness of the father and the willingness of the mother to "cover" for daughters when they break the rules.

A girl is expected to fulfill family duties well before her fifteenth birthday. The girl already knows house duties. The ritual can mark a transformation of appearance (the use of make-up and fashionable clothes), but the transformation is part of an ongoing process that has started well before fifteen. In this sense the fifteenth birthday celebration embodies a process of change rather than a clear-cut step from one irreversible stage to another. The *quinceañera* during her feast may receive a range of presents (perfumes, tights and make-up, and also teddy-bears or other stuffed animals) which mark a coexistence of childhood and adolescent elements. The language of a *mujercita* also changes: she can no longer use the jargon of street play and must avoid the use of uncontrolled, youthful expressions. However, this control is not perceived as a move away from childhood:

> Now it is necessary to know what one does and why one does it and to be able to decide. But I still feel like a child. We carry childhood within us and we never should lose it. For that reason I like to play with my little sisters (Angelica, a *quinceañera*).

The extent to which some elements of play and childhood are maintained after the age of fifteen depends on girls' personalities, their relations with the other sex, their roles within the family, and on the degree of family control. In this sense the ritual does not point to a linear evolution but to coexisting, multiple, and sometimes antithetic aspects of femaleness, and it does not just imprint a social status on a girl, but "brings out the social relations of which she . . . is composed" (Strathern 1993: 48).

Some mothers remarked to me that at this age daughters start to be more selfish towards their brothers and sisters. They become more helpful in the house, but at the same time start to carve out their own "private" space both metaphorically and physically; their "territory" may well be just one corner of a room, which is often shared with other sisters. Moreover, the process of becoming a *mujercita* takes place through becoming acquainted with a specific female knowledge—such as changes in female bodily shape and cycles—

which has to be kept from the other sex and must not be shared with brothers or fathers. The religious message of sexual purity connected to the ritual relates to this body of knowledge.

The Mass for a *quinceañera* is celebrated to thank God "de no haber fracasado." *Fracasar* means to break badly as a result of hitting or being hit. Metaphorically, it signifies becoming pregnant and therefore losing virginity, and implies that the girl's body is an unpenetrated whole. *Fracasar* takes place when this whole is seen as broken. However, *fracasar* is a redeemable state, as becoming a mother is valued in itself, irrespective of the fact of being married or not (Melhuus 1992: 175).

Through the symbolic values of the elements used in the feast, the ritual constructs an image of female "gentleness," "beauty," and "magic" outside of everyday reality. The dress and hairstyle of the *quinceañera*, the cushions and champagne glasses that she may receive from her godmothers, all refer to these conceptions of purity. The fifteenth birthday celebration, as the beginning of the time of illusion, thus suggests a whole female body celebrated in its integrity, unpenetrated by "reality"—or protected from penetration so as to enhance the status and reputation of the family.[11] This integrity should last until the wedding, because sexual intercourse and reproduction are part of that "reality" associated with the end of the "dreamed" female freedom, and with the subordination of a "broken body" to family control. This is the case with some single mothers in Polanco. Families react in various ways to pregnancies out of wedlock. If the father of the baby does not want to *reparar* ("mend") the situation by marrying the girl, she will turn to her family. Parents, and fathers especially, may react by banishing her from the family home while she is pregnant and sending her to some relative's house. However, after the birth of the child she is reaccepted into family life on condition that she accepts certain stringent limitations of her freedom.

If the time of "illusion" for a girl is related to ideas of enjoyment and male kindness during courtship, the representation of the time of "reality" is characterized by female suffering, male jealousy, and lack of care. Girls of fifteen know that the time of "reality" is associated with female hardship and male betrayal—even if they often say that they will marry a man who will not make their life miserable.

If the Catholic symbolism of the fifteenth birthday celebration relates to a girl's virginity, the girl herself may value the ritual experience for quite different reasons, because the reality of her life may be discordant with some of the symbolic meaning of the ritual. Such was the case with Tania, a pregnant girl who celebrated her fifteenth birthday and married a few months later. Everyone in her family, as well as the priest, knew of the situation but the celebration took place nonetheless, even if in a lower key than is usual. The *chambelano* was her fiancé and she danced the waltz just as any other *quinceañera*. She had daydreamed for so long about this feast that her pregnancy did not deter her from undertaking it. The celebration of the ritual of becoming a *mujercita* cannot be denied to a girl by the fact of being pregnant, even if unmarried pregnant women should not take part in public rituals (Arnold 1978). The experience of *being celebrated* in the ritual, and the enactment of daydreams, can be stronger than the symbolic message of virginal purity that the ritual embodies. In this case the "reality" of a female "broken" body coexisted with the representation of a time of "illusion" in which the body was still "unbroken."

Moore (1994*a*) has stressed that the representative aspect of gender—that is, the imaginative and performative dimension—needs to be re-represented and resignified through social action such as rituals. This is because the experience of the engendered body often resists social discourse, which imposes a regime of intelligibility of the body itself. The ritual of the fifteenth birthday feast and the time of "illusion" which the ritual initiates are also imaginative experiences in which gender categories are re-represented and sometimes resisted; they embody "fantasies" of identity which relate to certain forms of power and agency within and between gendered subjects (Moore 1994*b*: 66).

In conclusion, the *fiesta* of the fifteenth birthday celebration is, so to speak, a real experience about "illusory" time. The emphasis which the CEBs place on the meaning of communality tends to ignore the relevance which the drama and performance have for the unique goals of individuals (Parkin 1992: 17; Turner 1982). This aspect becomes central when the fifteenth birthday celebration fails to correspond to its socially and religiously approved meanings (as in Tania's example) and explains also why many *quinceañeras* decide to opt out of the communal ritual by celebrating their fifteenth birthdays in parishes outside Lomas de Polanco.

CELEBRATING OR NOT CELEBRATING

The fifteenth birthday is not celebrated by all girls in Lomas de Polanco. Its celebration—or omission—enhances different, sometimes conflicting, aspects of female identity as well as different class positions and their representations. If a family is keen to celebrate a daughter's fifteenth birthday, the feast can take place in various forms. The most expensive form involves the nuclear family, together with godparents and other members of the extended family, pooling resources to rent a ballroom. Although I heard of such occasions, I never observed one in Lomas de Polanco. Similar expenses are incurred if the *fiesta* is held in the village of origin of one or both of the *quinceañera's* parents. Opting to celebrate a life-crisis ritual in the village rather than in Lomas de Polanco not only informs the village of the status of the migrant family, but also reinforces a tie of belonging on the part of the offspring even if they were, as is often the case, born in the city. In these circumstances, the parents may express the wish that one day the *quinceañera* marries someone from the village. In other cases, the celebration may take place in the open air—perhaps on a farm that a relative or a godfather has put at the disposal of the family.

In most cases, the party is held in the family home in Lomas de Polanco and a stereo system and lighting are rented or a band is paid to play live music. However, if the family cannot afford the feast or is not keen on the celebration, the birthday may be celebrated with a generous meal at home between close relatives.

The main reason why some girls celebrate their Mass and others do not is economic: the cost of the whole feast varies, but if there is live music, it is at least around a million and a half pesos (around 500 U.S. dollars, before the peso's devaluation in 1994).[12] If the immediate family does not have the means, resources are pooled within the extended family; often godparents help to cover part of the cost, by paying for the dress, the food, or the music. Nonetheless, financial difficulties are not the only factor to prevent the celebration from taking place. Girls who do not celebrate the feast can be divided into two groups: those from households in straitened economic circumstances, and those who prefer to spend the money in a different way—such as saving to buy a small car.

The omission of the fifteenth birthday celebration by well-off families is a sign of distinction. Families such as the Ortega, whose members—both female and male—have achieved considerable educational and professional status and who are highly respected within the neighborhood, look down on the feast. The professional status of the Ortega sisters has put their relationships with men on a different footing. For this family, the celebration of the feast would not have been a sign of distinction, because the public recognition of the daughters' rights to have boyfriends was not a priority for them at the age of fifteen but only later, once they had finished their education. There was no need for their family to celebrate the fifteenth birthday feast to improve their status within the community; on the contrary, this would have lowered the family to a social level to which it did not want to belong. The decision of the Ortega family was an attempt at both individual and family emancipation from communal identity. The celebration of the *quinceañera* can thus be interpreted in two different ways. It is a demonstration of family status and prestige. However, it can also be regarded, especially by the middle classes, as a vulgar celebration which enhances aspects of female identity and sexuality with which they do not want to be associated.

Some girls attach great significance to the celebration of the Mass or to holding a family gathering; other girls privilege the importance of the feast—"their feast"—over the experience and the content of the Mass. Girls who have dropped out of school at an early age, and those who are still studying, tend to emphasize quite different meanings of the ritual. Girls at school are more protected by the family than girls who already work, and they often have to decide between studying or having a boyfriend (courtship on a regular basis occupies part of every evening). In the majority of cases, a girl's freedom of movement after the *quinceañera* is reduced, as she can see her boyfriend only in the presence of a third person such as a younger brother.

Milena, the fifteen-year-old daughter of Cuca and Juan—two active members of the Movimiento Familiar Cristiano (MFC), a relatively traditional Catholic group—had daydreamed about her fifteenth birthday celebration since she was twelve. Her parents encouraged her to undergo it. She dropped out of school because she was bored but had not yet found a job. Six months before her birthday Milena started to think seriously about the celebration. She looked at dresses, saved up a part of her weekly pocket money, and found a little job to help meet expenses. Milena had gone out with her boyfriend since she turned fourteen. Her parents insisted she only meet him in front of the house and did not go to *fiestas* with him. Since finding a boyfriend, she has dropped previous male friendships. Even her female friendships have been reduced, since she and her boyfriend criticize female gatherings as a source of unpleasant gossip. Milena spoke of her *quince* as the moment at which she will take "the right path": "Up to now I have felt confused. I can be led astray by friends. But after my fifteenth, I will be able to see what is more appropriate." The process of becoming a *mujercita* takes place through a new awareness of male intentions so that "you do not let them manipulate you, and you learn to choose" (Nubia). Milena herself did not trust her boyfriend to take her out on her own before her *quince*.

Like many girls in Lomas de Polanco, Milena was not sure that her family could afford the celebration until a few weeks beforehand. But, with the help of relatives and godparents, her feast was celebrated with a special attendance by some couples from the MFC. The attitude of Milena's mother towards her *quince* was a mixture of pride and worry. Cuca feared that Milena would get married too soon after her fifteenth birthday, because she had already been going out with her boyfriend for some time. Her concern was that "she would stick to the first," making the same mistake as her mother, who regretted having embarked upon married life so young and inexperienced.

Milena's power within the family changed visibly a few months after her feast. She was more often in charge of the housework. She used to play and argue with her younger sister, but now she called her *mi hija*, "my daughter," a term used to mark a status difference.[13] Milena behaved differently with her father too. She used to hug or kiss him when he left for work, but then her physical relation with him became more distant. She often complained that her brothers no longer took her out to *fiestas* because girls might think she was one of their girlfriends.

Sabrina, the first of four children of Alfonso—a co-ordinator of the CEBs as well as the MFC—did not think of celebrating her fifteenth birthday with a feast. Alfonso had to leave his job because of ill health. The household budget was tight, but priority was placed on investment in the children's education. Sabrina and her parents hoped she would eventually be able to attend university. Sabrina's parents' experience in the CEBs made them sensitive to the priority of the Mass over the feast:

> There is no need to spend so much for a feast. What is more important is the Mass in order to give thanks to God, and having a small family gathering. There are many people who get into debt to have a good feast, but it is better to spend on schooling (Elsa, Sabrina's mother).

The message was assimilated by the daughter, and Sabrina asked just to celebrate the Mass. She was aware that her father worked only part-time, and that her parents were doing their best to support her higher education. Sabrina had never had a secret sweetheart, but after her birthday she asked her father for permission to go out with a schoolmate. However, she clearly stated that she was not going to be distracted by him. Her energy and effort were focused on finishing her schooling, and, she hoped, going to university. She also wanted to save to buy a small car. She herself was surprised, a few weeks before her birthday, by the insistence of her parents (especially her father) that they celebrate her *quince años*. Alfonso was aware from his experience in the *Comunidades* that there was no need to spend money on this feast, and that other people in the parish would have understood his position. However, Sabrina was the first of his four children and the only daughter. For Alfonso, it was important that his daughter—towards whom, in Sabrina's words, he was extremely protective and jealous—should celebrate the feast. Her father was very strict with her and justified his insistence on the celebration by stating he wanted his daughter to have a nice memory of her *quince*; after all, Sabrina was his *consentida*, ("privileged one"). In the end, Sabrina was pleased to celebrate her feast—at home and on a reduced scale—because she felt the center of attention.

The cases of Ester and Julia, on the other hand, suggest that the relative importance of the Mass and *fiesta* is connected with the degree of family control over a girl's sexuality. Ester had been working since she was ten, and now worked as a shop-cleaner. She was not fully literate, but looked older than her years because she used make-up and tight clothes with confidence. Ester was born in a *casa chica*.[14] She has had a boyfriend since she was twelve, and went to *fiestas* with friends until late at night. Neighbors commented upon her hanging around with various male friends and her mother admitted that she could not "control" her very easily.

> She is very rebellious. Sometime I cannot bring her inside at ten, but at eleven . . . she wants to enjoy herself, but needs to realize that if she finds herself with something (i.e., pregnant), then I will be not responsible: she will be.

The godfather and sponsor of her fifteenth birthday celebration was supposed to be one of her former employers, but at the last minute he withdrew and contributed only some of the meat. So she borrowed a wedding dress from a friend, bought some shoes and paid for the music. After the feast, the family was absolutely impoverished and probably had to go without some meals, while the house looked run-down and badly maintained. This family spent more on the *fiesta* (they rented a live band) than other, better-off, families in Lomas de Polanco on similar occasions. For Ester, the Mass was not as important as the *fiesta* and the ball. However, she seemed disappointed at the way the feast turned out because there were some fights towards the end and the music was not as good as she expected. She also expressed disappointment that almost none of her extended family, who were expected to come, turned up to the *fiesta*.

The glamorous atmosphere of an "outstanding" day, in contrast to the daily life-style of her family, seemed to be Ester's strongest motivation for celebrating the *fiesta*. Her precocious habits, her relationship with her mother, and the family's careless housekeeping were negatively judged by their neighbors. She was not seen as having "honor," nor was her family. These were probably some of the reasons why the neighbors did not attend the feast. Ester's case shows an aspect of femaleness that claims freedom and pleasure, and rejects subordination to parental authority.

Juana seemed an opposite case. Her family's control over her was much stronger. She studied as an accountant and was not allowed to go out with friends to *fiestas*. She spent much of her time at home, and was described as very responsible by her family. She wore fashionable clothes and light make-up, but without being provocative. Juana had two older sisters and an older brother who pooled money to buy her a dress and sponsor the rental of a sound system and lighting equipment for the *fiesta*. Her father, a chief building worker, bought the necessaries for the party. Juana's *fiesta* was considered a success by her family and friends, even though it lacked live music. In contrast to Ester's case, the unity of Juana's family and its respectability in the eyes of neighbors contributed to a positive outcome.

Juana especially enjoyed the Mass and having all her family around her. After the celebration she described the intense emotion she felt at being near the altar and receiving her Mass. Now she wished, after her fifteenth, to have more responsibility as she was "not a child any more." She wanted to commit herself fully to her study and work. Her mother felt protective towards her, not because she mistrusted Juana but because of the boys who might deceive her. In her words: "if the girl has more than one boyfriend people talk badly about her. But the boy can have more than one girlfriend at the same time!"

In respecting her family's rules, and accepting the need to be protected from the danger of male sexual intentions, Juana—unlike Ester, who seemed to look for dangerous encounters—embodied the ideal symbolic meaning of the celebration of a *quinceañera*: submission, virginity, and control of the female body, which require "appropriate" dress, language, and social relationships with the same and the opposite sex.

The cases of Ester and Juana show that this rite of passage entails tensions between different aspects of male and female sexualities. Female sexuality should be controlled, kept away from male "wandering" (i.e., philandering). But at the same time virility is measured in relation to a man's capacity to attract and dominate the opposite sex (Wade 1994: 129). Female sexuality—when manifested in circumstances of male "wandering"—becomes threatening to family order because it is deceitful and uncontrolled (Martin 1990: 478). Yet some girls may actively look for sexual encounters. The fifteenth birthday celebration, then, becomes a theater for different and often opposed female identities, as is the case in some other rites of passage related to female puberty (Wilson 1980: 621).

The cases of Milena, Sabrina, Juana, and Ester show that the same ritual can enhance different aspects of womanhood in relation to the life-styles and religious beliefs of girls' families. A celebration held by a family involved in the CEBs (such as the family of Sabrina) tends to be less ostentatious than one held by those only involved in more "traditional" Catholic groups (for instance, the family of Milena), because savings may be invested in a daughter's education or in the acquisition of valuable commodities, rather than in the *fiesta*.

CONCLUSION

As we have seen, the fifteenth birthday celebration has acquired new meanings in the language of the CEBs. These new meanings emphasize the priority of communal identity over family and individual "protagonism." Priests and their assistants criticize "traditional" *fiestas* as expressions of an idea of the family as a "competitive" unit which wishes to increase its social status.

The performance of (and, indeed, the failure to perform) the fifteenth birthday celebration clearly carries a meaning of social differentiation and transformation of female social status; however, the ritual also constitutes an important moment in the process of female identity and self-perception because it opens up a time of negotiation within the family concerning control over, and definition of, the female sexual body. This phase ends with married life, when the time of "illusion"—the time of suspended disbeliefs—can be extended no longer. CEBs' discourse—which often de-emphasizes issues of gender hierarchy in favor of ideals of the communality of the "poor"—fails to a certain extent to grasp the importance of the body and embodied experience in the ritual in the formation of female identity. Instead, it emphasizes the roots of the ritual in a "mythical" past which, rather than stressing the singularity of specific villages or *ranchos*, enhances the communality of memory.

The drama of the ritual constructs the female body through images of virginity and metaphors of the body as a vessel to be preserved intact. The time of "illusion," which begins with the ritual, indicates the new complexity of a dimension of female identity. Girls acquire new responsibilities towards their families, which their wish to engage in courtship demands a loosening of family control. Girls are symbolically handed over to the male domain, but they also experience self-empowerment in the ritual. After the ritual, however, their freedom of action is often reduced, as well as their autonomy in relation to the male domain—this tight control being one of the causes of early marriage. The ritual thus expresses discontinuities as well as continuities (Crapanzano 1992) in the process of becoming a *mujercita*.

The ritual cannot be reduced, as the CEBs' discourse implies, to its functions of family status differentiation and "consumption." On the other hand, the ritual cannot be fully understood if we focus only on its symbolic level: on the ways it marks sexual boundaries, and helps to construct the female body as a vessel which needs to be defended from male philandering. The ritual is a performative act, an experience which may or may not be part of the process of creation of female self-identity. Indigenous exegeses of the ritual (and, indeed, of reasons for foregoing it) need to be understood within the context of particular sets of family relations—which are very heterogeneous—and also differing contexts of religious discourse and perceptions of class and status. For a wide range of economic and other considerations affect peoples' decisions about whether to celebrate the ceremony and, if so, on what scale.

NOTES

The material in this article is drawn from my thesis (Napolitano 1995), based on eight months of fieldwork between the summer of 1990 and the spring of 1992, funded by University of London Scholarship Fund. I am in great debt to Richard Fardon, Peter Wiley, John Gledhill, and Stephen Hugh-Jones for their insightful comments on early versions of this article.

1. The CEBs are Catholic groups for biblical reflection organized at street level based on "residential vicinity and local knowledge" (Banck 1989: 13). Following liberation theology teaching, they aim to raise consciousness so as to act against social injustice and improve solidarity and living conditions among the underprivileged.

They are organized at the level of the parish, but are also part of regional and national networks.

2. A *colonia popular* is a low-income neighborhood. Its degree of economic homogeneity can vary but the term *popular* refers always to its class composition.

3. Many factors have influenced migration to Guadalajara, such as the shift to cash crops cultivation, the freezing of official prices for basic agricultural products, and the concentration of services and economic activities (Orozco 1989), but we should not forget that, in many cases, individual's reasons for migration may override collective household interests (Melhuus 1992: 62).

4. My data were collected before the dramatic devaluation of the *peso* in December 1994. However, the economic crisis of the early 1980s—connected to the fall of prices—had already resulted in a decrease in the buying power of factory wages, and increased informalization of the market economy and a higher female participation. Nevertheless, Lomas de Polanco is a special case, as it is becoming a "center" for the periphery since a huge and well stocked street market takes place twice a week; this attracts customers from surrounding areas and has pushed up house prices, especially around the street market, obliging many families renting and living on very low incomes to move out into less expensive neighborhoods.

5. LeVine has pointed out in a study carried out among women in Cuernavaca that this feast has been celebrated by working-class families since the 1950s (1993: 60).

6. There may be a correspondence between the ideal number of *damas, chambelanos,* and the girl. Fourteen people (seven *chambelanos* and seven *damas*) could stand for the fourteen years, while the *quinceañera* represents the fifteenth year/person. The stress is therefore on singularity: she represents the odd number, individuality, that which stands out unmatched.

7. *Fiestas de quiceñeras* which go on after this time are criticized by the CEBs-inclined clergy and their assistants in Polanco, because they go beyond the aim of a family gathering.

8. I refer to groups such as the Adoración Nocturna and the Vela del Santisimo which promote an image of the Virgin Mary that stresses endurance, encompassing love, and eternal forgiveness.

9. Padre Rodolfo has introduced a special moment into the Mass for the "fifteenth" of girls celebrated in Santa Magdalena. During this, the girls have to hold each others' hands and recite a prayer:

> Lord, I give you thanks for these fifteen years of my life that you have granted me . . . for my parents, my brothers . . . and for the love with which they have educated me . . . I love and admire this world, that is the work of your hands, the sun, the flowers, the stars, the water, the wind and what is born and grows on this earth. I recognize that the society I join today, with enhanced consciousness, has many negative aspects . . . nevertheless there are many good people ready to give me a hand to follow the good path.

10. The girls are made to reaffirm, as in confirmation, the baptismal vow of the rejection of Satan.

11. Collier, discussing the changes in female self-conception in an Andalusian village, writes: "The status and reputation of the family thus rests on the degree to which its women are protected from penetration—by a woman's sense of sexual shame, by being locked away and/or by the courage of family men in repelling seducers" (1986: 101).

12. The basic costs are those of the dress and shoes of the *quinceañera*; the food (normally *birria*—a meat dish—beans and *tortillas*), soft drinks and beer; the fee for the Mass, which varies from church to church; and the charge for the rental of music equipment.

13. "Mi hija" is also used between adult women who are not blood relatives and can

be used by husbands to their wives. Although an affectionate term, it evokes a status difference between speaker and addressee.

14. A *casa chica* is a single female parent household formed by a man in an extramarital relationship. The father of Ester lives in another state of Mexico and rarely comes to see his six sons and daughters.

REFERENCES

Alvarez, S. 1990. Women's Participation in Brazilian "People's Church": a critical appraisal. *Fem. Stud.* 16, 381–409.

Arizpe, L. 1977. Women in the Informal Sector: The Case of Mexico City. *Signs* 3, 24–37.

Arnold, M. 1978. Celibes, Mothers and Church Cockroaches: Religious Participation of Women in a Mexican Village. In *Women in ritual and symbolic roles* (eds.) J. Hoch-Smith and A. Spring. New York: Plenum Press.

Banck, G. 1989. Cultural dilemmas Behind the Strategy of Brazilian Neighborhood Movements and Catholic discourse. Paper presented at the University of Texas, Austin.

Beneria, L. and M. Roldan. 1987. *The crossroad of class and gender.* Chicago: University of Chicago Press.

Burdick, J. 1992. Rethinking the Study of Social Movements: The Case of Christian Base Communities in Urban Brazil. In *The making of social movements in Latin America* (eds.) A. Escobar and S. Alvarez, Boulder: Westview Press.

———. 1994. The progressive Catholic Church in Latin America: Going Voices or Listening to Voices? *Lat. Am. Res. Rev.* 29, 184–97.

Cardenas Gonzalez, H. 1987. "Los quince años": ritos y rectos pars la confirmación? *Teo Cateq.* 21, 115–22.

Collier, J. 1986. From Mari to Modern Woman: The Material Basis of Marianismo and Its Transformation in a Spanish Village. *Am. Ethnol.* 13, 100–107.

Crapanzano, V. 1992. Rite of Return. In *Hermes' dilemma and Hamlet's desire.* Cambridge MA: Harvard University Press.

Craske, N. 1933. Women's Political Participation in Colonias Populares in Guadalajara Mexico. In *Viva women and popular protest in Latin American Catholicism* (eds) S. Radcliffe and S. Westwood. London, New York: Routledge.

Díaz, M. 1966. *Tonalá: conservatorism, responsibility, and authority in a Mexican town.* Berkeley: University of California Press.

Díaz-Guerrero, R. 1975. *Psychology of the Mexican: culture and personality.* Austin: University Texas Press.

Drogus, C. 1990. Reconstructing the Feminine: Women in Sao Paulo's CEBs. *Arch. Sci. Sociale Relig.* 71, 63–74.

Foweraker, J. 1995. *Theorizing social movements.* London: Pluto Press.

Fromm, E. and M. Maccoby. 1970. *The social character of a Mexican village.* Englewood Cliffs: Prentice-Hall.

Gennep, A. van. 1977 (1909). *Rites of passage.* London: Routledge & Kegan Paul.

Gutmann, M. C. 1996. *The meanings of macho: being a man in Mexico City.* Berkeley: University of California Press.

Hewitt, W. E. 1991. *Base Christian Communities and social change in Brazil.* Lincoln, NE: University of Nebraska Press.

Kemper, R. V. 1977. *Migration and adaptation: Tzintzuntzan migration to Mexico City.* Beverly Hills: Sage.

Levine, D. H. 1985. Continuities in Colombia. *J. Lat. Am. Stud.* 17, 295–317.

———. 1992. *Popular voices in Latin American Catholicism.* Princeton: Princeton University Press.

LeVine, S. 1993. *Dolor y alegria: women and social change in urban Mexico*. Madison: University of Wisconsin Press.

Logan, K. 1988. Women, Political Activity and Empowerment in Latin American Urban Movements. In *Urban life: readings in urban anthropology* (eds.) G. Gmelch and W. P. Zennier. Prospect Heights: Waveland Press.

Lomnitz, L. and M. Perez-Lizaur 1987. *A Mexican elite family, 1920–1980*. Princeton: University Press.

Martin, J. 1990. Motherhood and Power: The Production of a Woman's Culture of Politics in a Mexican Community. *Am. Ethnol.* 17, 470–90.

Melhuus, M. 1992. Morality, Meaning and Change in a Mexican Community. Thesis, Department and Museum of Anthropology, University of Oslo.

Moore, H. 1994a. Gender Identity and Consciousness. Paper presented at the ASA conference "Questions of consciousness," University of St. Andrews.

———. 1994b. *A passion for difference*. Cambridge: Polity Press.

Morfin Otero, M. G. 1979. Anÿlisis de la legislación urbana, su aplicaón y consecuencias: el caso de Lomas de Pelanco, Guadalajara. Thesis, University of Guadalajara.

Napolitano, V. 1995. Self and Identity in a "Colonia Popular" of Guadalajara, Mexico. Thesis, University of London.

Nash, J. and H. Safa. 1976. *Class and gender in Latin America*. South Hadley, MA: Bergin and Garvey.

——— and ———. 1986. *Women and change in Latin America*. South Hadley, MA: Bergin and Garvey.

Orozco, J. 1989. La agroindustria de granos en la Zona Metropolitana de Guadalajara y su incidencia en la agricultura y la emigración rural de Jalisco. Thesis, University of Guadalajara.

Parkin, D. 1992. Ritual as Spatial Direction and Bodily Division. In *Understanding rituals* (ed.) D. de Coppet. London: Routledge.

Romanucci-Ross, L. 1973. *Conflict, violence and morality in a Mexican village*. Palo Alto: National University Press.

Sanchez VanDyck de Levy, M. 1979. Le phénomène de fractionnements populaires a Guadalajara, Jalisco, Mexique. Thesis, Ecole des Hautes Etudes en Sciences Sociales, Paris.

Strathern, M. 1993. Making Incomplete. In *Carved Flesh/cast selves* (eds.) V. Broch-Due and T. Bleig. Oxford: Berg.

Turner, V. W. 1974. *Dramas, fields and metaphors*. Ithaca, London: Cornell University Press.

———. 1982. *From ritual to theatre*. New York: Performing Art Journal Publications.

Wade, P. 1994. Man and Hunter: Gender and Violence in Music and Drinking Contexts in Colombia. In *Sex and violence* (eds.) P. Harvey and P. Gow. London, New York: Routledge.

Westwood, S. and S. Radcliffe. 1993. Gender, Racism and the Politics of Identities in Latin America. In *Viva: women and popular protest in Latin America* (eds.) S. Radcliffe and S. Westwood. London, New York: Routledge.

Wilson, D. 1980. Rituals of First Menstruation in Sri Lanka. *Man* (N.S.) 15, 603–25.

Performances of Race, Culture, Class, and Religion in the Somerville Community

Sara Arcaya

INTRODUCTION

"Más que tradición religiosa, es una tradición del pueblo, ve, y claro cada tradición del pueblo y cada cultura trae consigo lo que toda la vida vivieron," according to Daisy Gómez, this is the *quinceañera*. The *quinceañera* is at once a tradition in a community—a reminder of its depth and history—while still an ever-changing celebration. It is a tradition of the people, a lived experience that evolves with those who practice it. This paper is the culmination of seven interviews with members of the Somerville, Massachusetts, Latino community and is one part of an ongoing project to record and make available that community's oral history.

Somerville is a city that lies along the Mystic River, five miles north of Boston. Most Tufts students think of Somerville as Davis Square, which is a ten-minute walk from campus. However, a short drive through Winter Hill and into East Somerville reveals quite a different community. Rather than seeing working class white residents whose Somerville ties extend back generations, or Tufts alumnae who have found jobs in nearby Cambridge, one is more likely to meet Salvadorans who have immigrated to the U.S. within the last twenty-five years. Restaurants like Tapatío and Los Paisanos are the significant places rather than the Joshua Tree and Starbucks. And the dominant language shifts from English to Spanish.

Somerville's predominately Salvadoran Latino population began to grow in the 1980s, when Central America experienced violent civil wars in three countries—Nicaragua, Guatemala, and El Salvador. Elena Letona, Cambridge

Sara Arcaya: "Performance of Race, Culture, Class and Religion in the Somerville Community," research paper presented at Tufts University as part of the course Urban Borderlands 2004 and the Cambridge/Somerville Oral Latino History Project, December 18, 2004.

community organizer at Centro Presente, refers to this immigration wave as an "exodus," claiming that between 1990 and 2000 the Salvadoran community in Massachusetts grew 139 percent. According to "Who Are New England's Immigrants?" close to one in three Somerville residents are foreign born, most of whom are Salvadoran or Brazilian (Borgos and Mammie 2004). Excluded under the U.S.'s Refugee Act of 1980, Salvadorans existed in a sort of limbo with regards to their political status—provisionally protected under temporary protected status, settlement, or workers' visas. By 1986 Somerville joined about twenty other cities that pledged to protect illegal immigrants fleeing Central America's civil wars, proclaiming itself a Sanctuary City. As Elaina Letona explains, Salvadorans in Massachusetts, as other immigrant communities, are not organized around geography, but around ethnicity. Many Salvadorans, because of Somerville's willingness to accept them regardless of their official immigration status, established roots in the city, making it more feasible for friends, families, and even entire communities to join.

A Tufts University class now in its third year, Urban Borderlands, introduced me to this community. The goal of this anthropology class is to document the oral history of Somerville Latinos and to teach students about conducting qualitative research through one-on-one interviews. The fall 2004 class is looking at the arrival and integration of Latinos into Somerville through eight research topics including that of businesspeople, religious life, and youth programs, all co-occurring with my own study on *quinceañeras*. While many students at Tufts can basically get by without descending "the hill" for four years, Urban Borderlands forces students to learn by experience. The class brings students into the community, allowing them to understand first hand the local politics, social issues, and customs. Little or none of this would otherwise make headlines at Tufts. The class met several times in the community, working in special partnership with The Welcome Project, an advocacy agency run by Nelson Salazar. Located in Somerville's Mystic Public Housing Development, The Welcome Project has dedicated itself to serving immigrant populations and facilitating their integration into Somerville since 1987. Students from the Urban Borderlands class were paired with high school students connected to The Welcome Project in order to conduct research and gain entrance into the Somerville Latino community.

My partner, Bianca Salazar, daughter of Nelson Salazar, is currently a junior at Somerville Charter High School. Bianca was especially helpful for a number of reasons: Bianca speaks Spanish fluently and knows her community. She largely inspired this research topic and agreed to let me interview her. In one of my first meetings with Bianca she described her *quinceañera*, which took place two years earlier. She was still excited about it. I wondered what purpose the *quinceañera* served on the community level, why it continues to thrive across borders and cultures, how it has affected Somerville, and how Somerville has affected it.

When the Urban Borderland reports are assembled into a comprehensive study of Somerville's Latino population, many chapters will reveal a community largely excluded from Somerville proper. It faces constant discrimination, has virtually no political representation, and has low home ownership rates. To be accurate, the book will also need to reflect the positive aspects that make a cohesive community. This chapter would reveal everyday life for Latinos in Somerville, what they value, and how these values translate into cultural events.

One such traditional celebration is the quinceañera, a coming of age ceremony for fifteen-year-old Latinas and Latin Americans. Because of the economic, racial, and cultural diversity among these societies, the *quinceañera* can take many forms. It most typically involves, however, both a religious and social ceremony in which the honoree gives thanks to God, the Virgin Mary, her family, and her social circle for having brought her thus far in life. While the quinceañera has often been compared to the Sweet Sixteens and Debutante Balls of Anglo Americans, C.C.D. director Daisy Gómez insists that it has nothing to do with these other coming of age celebrations. It is instead a Hispanic religious event that sustains and invigorates communities and takes unique shape in the context of Somerville. This project is truly a collaborative one involving the Urban Borderlands class, Bianca Salazar, The Welcome Project, and greater Somerville.

OBJECTIVES

The goal of this paper is to look from an anthropological perspective at the long held tradition of *quinceañeras* in the context of Somerville's Latino community. Each interview, though broad in its subject matter, was guided by the overarching question: what purpose does the quinceañera serve in Somerville? Their community and unique places in society have of course influenced the respondents; their statements reflect their views alone and should not be interpreted as reflections of all of Somerville. The report explores how the narrators' performance of the tradition reflects their unique locations in society, as members of a marginalized and economically disadvantaged group with close ties to their sending nations. Hardly passive participants, Somerville Latinos have collectively influenced the shape of this longstanding cultural tradition, one that now incorporates local values and bicultural influences. It also reflects how the community perceives itself.

Narrators' statements were largely in tune with Saint Benedict's C.C.D. director, Daisy Gómez's assertion. The *quinceañera* is a lived experience that moves with the people who practice it—something that is at once constant, a reminder of the depth and history of one's culture, and still dynamic, reflecting the daily reality of Somerville Latinos. The following report details those elements of the *quinceañera* that the narrators found were of notable significance to them. It also contends that the *quinceañera* continues in Somerville because it actively creates and strengthens the community.

METHODOLOGY

During two and a half months, I conducted seven interviews for this project, three in conjunction with Bianca Salazar, my high school contact. The first few interviews were contained within the Welcome Project network, but as one narrator introduced me to the next, and so on, I began extending my reach into the greater community. The topics of each interview included the religious significance of a *quinceañera*, the economic factors involved, and the concepts of beauty and feminity the custom reveals. Each interview took place in Somerville—in the Welcome Project, narrators' homes, at a local business, and in Saint Benedict's parish—and lasted between forty-five and sixty minutes. I entered each interview with a set of questions specific to my narrator and his or her role in the *quinceañera* tradition, conducting the conversation in either Spanish or English, as per his or her preference. Most interviews took the form of personal stories much more than a strict question and answer exchange. The narrators all signed consent forms giving me rights to their interviews for the purpose of this oral history project.

As the project progressed, my focus became narrower. I began adding questions, asking narrators to comment on concepts and trends explained in past interviews, and about conclusions I was generating. My focus population also began to take shape as I realized that at least six out of seven of my narrators were part of Saint Benedict's congregation. Given that religion is especially tied to the Somerville Salvadoran *quinceañera*, the Saint Benedict's connection became a significant element of my report and tied narrators' experiences to one institution and religious community.

Since this project only covered one semester, I was limited as to the amount of material I could gather. There is certainly more work to be done. There are many other communities within the Somerville Latino population, as well as countless other areas of which one could conduct research. This is a population largely ignored by the public eye, though with a wealth of experiences and knowledge to share. At the conclusion of this report, I will suggest further areas of study.

LIST OF NARRATORS

Heidy Castro is twenty-one years old and of Salvadoran descent. She was born in Cambridge, Massachusetts, in 1983 and was raised in Somerville. She currently has a two-year-old son and lives with her family a short distance from The Welcome Project. Heidy is an active parishioner at Saint Benedict's and was introduced to me by the religious director there, Daisy Gómez.

Milagro Garcia, owner of Doña Milagro's in Somerville, emigrated from El Salvador on May 4, 1988. Doña Milagro's specializes in women's formalwear, selling dresses for weddings, *quinceañeras*, and graduation celebrations. She draws an entirely Latino clientel and has participated in the oral history project once before, for a study called "The Latino Business Community in Somerville, MA" by David Pistrang and Emily Chasan. I do not know whether Milagro Garcia attends Saint Benedict's Parish.

Daisy Gómez immigrated to the United States in 1957 from Cuba. She has been living in Dorchester, Massachusetts, for over forty years, though is closely tied to the Somerville community. As director of religious education and assistant to the pastor at Saint Benedict's, she is in charge of almost all projects the parish undertakes with respect to the Somerville Hispanic community.

Berta Guevara is a Salvadoran woman who immigrated to the United States in 1993 and has since become an active member of the Saint Benedict's congregation. Berta is an instructor at the religious school, a lector during Sunday mass, and takes care of many administrative tasks.

Bianca Salazar is seventeen years old and currently a junior at the Somerville Charter High School. She is a Salvadoran Latina who had her *quinceañera* two years prior to this report. Both my high school partner and one of my seven narrators, Bianca was the first to provide the essential perspective of a *quinceañera* honoree, giving my study both depth and direction. She also suggested that I get to know Saint Benedict's and interview the CCD director.

Nelson Salazar, father of Bianca Salazar, is founder and director of Somerville's The Welcome Project. He immigrated to the United States from Sonsonante, El Salvador, in 1980. Nelson Salazar and The Welcome Project have been working with Urban Borderlands for two years now, pairing high school and college students to learn about and document the Somerville Latino population's oral history.

Jessica Tejada is seventeen years old, of Salvadoran descent, and a junior at the Somerville Charter High School. She is connected to the Urban Borderlands class through The Welcome Project and has been interviewing the Somerville Latino business community as part of a study entitled, "The Latino Business Community and the City of Somerville."

*"From girl to señorita. It was a way to present them to society—
the upper-class society"*

SYMBOLS OF WOMANHOOD
IN THE *QUINCEAÑERA*

While the focus of this paper lies in exploring the current purpose of the quinceañera in Somerville, a basic understanding of its roots gives insight into the tradition's current form. According to Nelson Salazar, *quinceañeras* came to the Americas with the Spaniards, who had adopted the tradition from the French. Although Mr. Salazar attributes the tradition to Spain, not all sources agree. There is apparently no conclusive evidence of this exchange. "Quinceañera presentations are unknown in Spain, and even in the sixteenth century court presentations were more akin to . . . presentation balls of particular groups, like fraternal organizations or to social events, like debutante balls," (Cantú 1999) the religious ceremony sets *quinceañeras* apart from these secular functions. Others like Norma E. Cantú have claimed, though this did not come up in any of my interviews, that at least some portion of the *quinceañera* can be traced back to indigenous roots. She says that while the pendant typically given to an honoree on her fifteenth birthday and blessed during the religious ceremony symbolizes "coming-of-age, it also functions as an identity marker that focuses her attention on her cultural heritage and establishes a direct link to her indigenous past" (Cantú 2002). Regardless of the *quinceañera*'s first incorporation into Latin/o cultures, it now consistently signals coming of age, in both a social and a religious sense.

Traditionally, *quinceañeras* signal a female's transformation, "from girl to señorita. It was a way to present them to society—the upper-class society," Mr. Salazar says. Although the Salazars are by no means wealthy, he says that *quinceañeras* "became a tradition for a lot of us." Given that Somerville's Salvadoran population is quite recent, working class, and still establishing itself in the city, the tradition has veered from its original presentation of a girl to society. Storeowner Milagro Garcia believes that now only Brazilians maintain this perspective in Somerville. Salvadorans and many other Latin American groups, she said, place greater emphasis on the more general concept of coming of age. One honoree, Heidy Castro, similarly acknowledged the social connotation of the *quinceañera* and a young woman's presentation to society. She, however, places higher value on the way that it presents a young woman to the parish and to God. It is as if she is "entregando su juventud a Dios—una juventud sana," (giving her youth to God, her healthy youth), through the religious ceremony, Heidy explained. Coming of age in a specifically religious context, however, will be treated in a later chapter.

The celebration also entails a secular concept of coming of age and reflects an infusion of cultural markers of this maturity. Milagro Garcia indicates one such marker, the crown. Mexican girls, she asserts, signal personal growth as they enter the church wearing a "corona de adolescente" and leave wearing a "corona de señorita," to signal that they are ready for suitors and have entered womanhood—but that's another culture, she clarified. Symbolizing this transformation into a señorita, Heidy's father, once they arrived at Saint Anthony's Church for her party, ceremonially, before all of the guests, removed her flat shoes and replaced them with high heels. She also pointed out that some mothers give their daughters a doll for the last time on the *quinceañera* as a keepsake. Though Bianca did not incorporate either of these traditions into her quinceañera, she too believes the event marks coming of age saying, "It was pretty much saying that now I had become a young lady, that I was entering high school, and that I was no longer a child." All narrators mentioned that the *quinceañera* symbolizes one's passage from youth into womanhood, though their concepts of womanhood certainly differ.

In describing their understanding of womanhood, Bianca and Heidy placed special emphasis on responsibility. As a teenage female now ready to have boyfriends, Bianca learned she would have to respect her body as the church preached. Berta Guevara, a lector at Saint Benedict's Parish, meets with most honorees to talk about such sexual transformations before their quinceañera. She stresses that while they have matured, honorees have not quite entered into womanhood but have grown from niña (little girl) to jóven (youth). Warning that they are still young and especially vulnerable, Ms. Guevara says that Somerville youth need to respect their bodies and demand that same respect from others. Heidy came to reflect on this concept of womanhood when asked how she might prepare a *quinceañera* if she were to have a daughter. For it to be a success, Heidy imagines, her daughter would have to understand what it means to be a good woman, to be dependable, and to care for herself. A good woman, Heidy defines as someone who follows her own mother's example, even in her absence; a good woman behaves herself, and continues to make herself better, moving forward each day. Heidy spoke further about the responsibilities that one assumes as a woman, saying that she must leave her dolls behind and realize that she has to depend on herself instead of her parents. Parents, Heidy says, have this same concept of womanhood. They believe they should be able to leave their daughter alone by age fifteen; upon return, the house should be in order and their daughter should have prepared dinner for the family. In Heidy's experience, the *quinceañera* gave her more self-confidence and did signal her shift in familial roles to that of a second caretaker.

Milagro Garcia, as a storeowner who deals with numerous *quinceañeras* every year, portrayed a similarly consistent, even fixed concept of womanhood. She says that cultural values and concepts of maturity easily transfer from one generation to the next. "Los papas son los que impulsan los valores morales y a los quince años los papas son los que mandan," (parents drive the moral values [inherent in this tradition], and at fifteen years of age it is still the parents that rule). Although Ms. Garcia sees symbolic significance in the *quinceañera* and its traditional signal of one's entrance into womanhood, she certainly distinguishes between a fifteen-year-old and a full-fledged adult. Still Ms. Garcia placed continuous emphasis on the way that culture passes seamlessly from one generation to the next. In fact, she contends that there is little difference between the performance of quinceañeras in El Salvador and in Somerville, Massachusetts. "Casi es lo mismo . . . casi todos tienen el mismo concepto [de pasar a la adolescencia]," (it is almost the same . . . almost everyone has the same concept [of a girl's passage into adolescence]), she assured me. According to Ms. Garcia, whether one is from the Caribbean, North, Central, or South America the *quinceañera* means the same thing—there is no difference in the way that girls understand coming of age across cultural and national landscapes. Surprised at this apparent rigid cultural concept of coming of age and stagnant understanding of culture, I asked Ms. Garcia to expand on this idea. With respect to the quinceañera, it is as if all Latin Americans share one culture, she states, "como si fuéramos de la misma, casi tienen las mismas cultural en ese aspecto de las quinceañeras. A veces el sistema americano usa el dieciséis y no quince." Sometimes in the United States they celebrate the sixteenth birthday, however, she clarified.

It is important to take into account Ms. Garcia's relationship to the *quinceañera*. Owner of a Somerville specialty store, Doña Milagro's, Ms. Garcia interacts with a select population around the *quinceañera* and has a strictly Latina clientele. It may be that the girls who look for dresses in stores like Doña Milagro's happen to share a more consistent set of values with their parents, while others who shop at mainstream chain stores find bicultural influences to be truer to their experiences. It is also worth qualifying that Somerville's Salvadoran community is relatively new. Another look at the values embedded within the *quinceañera* after two or three more generations of the community's integration into Somerville will certainly show changes in the performance and greater influence from dominant cultures.

"Yes! I am Latina ... Yes! I just had my quinceañera!"

QUINCEAÑERAS IMPACTING IDENTITY

The *quinceañera,* as any cultural practice, is jointly negotiated and created, constantly influenced by the context in which it occurs. As a ceremonial rite of passage so tied to the honoree's identity, her language, race, self-perception, sexuality, and class all come to influence this cultural performance. In 2002, Jessica Tejada celebrated her *quinceañera* with a religious mass at Saint Benedict's and a party to follow at the Welcome Project. Jessica's bilingual sermon reflects a bicultural influence inherent in the performance. According to Jessica, besides her relatives who traveled from Lawrence, Massachusetts, for the celebration, there were also "a lot of young people" and this changed the dynamics of the sermon. The priest judged the guests' language ability and code switched depending on his intended audience. When the priest spoke directly to the younger people, he used Spanglish, and sometimes English. But, Jessica recalls, "When he had to make a point for everyone, he spoke in Spanish." Everyone attending Jessica's mass was Latino, but the priest recognized the diversity in language ability across Latino populations and adapted his sermon accordingly.

His willingness to code switch in this most traditional of Latino customs seems to signal his acceptance of (and accommodation to) the fact that Latinos exist on a cultural and linguistic continuum. They have had varying experiences in acquiring or learning English, though neither one is more authentically Latino than the other. While English often resonates more with the younger generation, Spanish still serves as a meeting point for this Somerville community.

Heidy, also an American born Salvadoran, feels this same bicultural influence as Jessica, in her daily life. The rule has always been, Heidy said in an interview, that she hears, speaks, and writes Spanish inside the house. The outside could teach her English, but inside the house was a place to experience Salvadoran culture. Both Heidy's grandmother and great-grandmother cultivated Salvadoran culture in the Castro house by passing down traditions like making tortillas. In part due to their influence, Heidy reflects, "Yo me siento mas salvadoreña que Estados Unidos," (I feel more Salvadoran than American). When she was young, Heidy remembers looking at fifteen year olds celebrating their birthdays and told her parents that she too wanted to have a *quinceañera.*

Reflecting back, on that celebration, Heidy says that the *quinceañera* strengthened her sense of community and brought her closer to those that attended. Many people who attended her party were adults that she had never spoken to before and only knew through her parents. A girl opens herself to the community through the *quinceañera,* Heidy explained. The *quinceañera* did not act as her presentation to society in that she was now ready to marry and be courted, but rather as a community builder. Heidy found that having a quinceañera enhanced her status within the Latino community, making boys and adults alike take notice of her and respect her as a young woman. While Heidy's life has always reflected a fusion of American and Salvadoran cultures, the *quinceañera* helped to bring her closer to that Salvadoran community of which she always knew she was a part but to which she had not been formally introduced.

Jessica views the *quinceañera* in a similar light, emphasizing its communal purpose. She describes her dance with her father as the most special moment of the night, and happily remembers how the other guests watched from afar, blowing bubbles around the pair. Afterwards she made sure that everyone danced to the DJ's reggae, reggaetón, and bachata. "It wasn't just a party for me," she reflects, "I was glad because I felt like everyone had fun and not just me." For Jessica, this event allowed her to celebrate a period of growth in her life, but it was a community and family event as well.

While Heidy and Jessica note that the *quinceañera* deepened their relationship to the Latino community and status within, for Bianca Salazar the way the event changed how others see her Latina identity was also important. Conscious of the fact that her light skin could lead others to label her as White, Bianca was especially excited to have a *quinceañera*, which she considers a marker of Latinidad. Bianca explains, "Seeing that people tend to think I'm white kinda made me be like, 'Yes! I'm a Latina.' I can go into school saying, 'Yes, I just had my quinceañera.' And everyone would be like 'Oh, so what's *that*?' And I'd be like 'Oh, it's a Latin thing.'" Bianca feels frustrated when others neglect to acknowledge her Latinidad and immersion in Somerville's Latino community, mistaking her for White. Despite the lived experiences that contradict this rigid definition, White and Latina are often seen as mutually exclusive terms in the United States. Bianca's experiences are indicative of race's fluid nature and how categories of White and Latina can simultaneously exist. Therefore the actual performance of the *quinceañera*, served as something tangible that Bianca could identify as Latino culture for the outside world so tempted to categorize her. While Bianca's concept of Salvadoran culture or Latinidad cannot actually be defined by one cultural performance, for her, the custom sufficed to silence those who might question her identity. Bianca concludes, "So it makes me feel proud of myself being able to say [I celebrated my *quinceañera*]—unlike when people'd be like, 'So, are you White?' It's like, 'No, I'm not. I might look it, but I'm not.' So, it feels pretty good." For Bianca, the performance came to serve as proof that her light skin was no indication of her ethnicity—Bianca was a Salvadoran Latina. Jessica, in contrast, did not see her *quinceañera* as a rite of passage into the Latino community or as a symbol of her Latinidad. Rather, it stood for her self-development and valued family traditions.

Ian F. Hany Lopez's, "The Mean Streets of Social Race" illuminates the way that race has shaped individuals like Bianca and Jessica, who navigate their Latina identities and connect with the *quinceañera* in very different ways. According to Lopez, three elements combine to form one's racial identity: chance, context, and choice. Chance, he states, is something unchangeable such as one's appearance and ancestry; by chance, both girls are Salvadoran though with very different shades of skin reflecting their distinct ancestry. Context is "the social setting in which races are recognized, constructed, and contested," (153) like Somerville, Massachusetts. And finally choice reflects the power one has over her racial identity in various contexts. While Bianca can pass as White, in cases where she can assert that she is a person of color, she does. Lopez assures,

> [Some] people do choose to jump races, and their ability to do so dramatically demonstrates the element of choice in the micromechanics of race. It also demonstrates . . . [choices] about racial identity do not occur on neutral ground, but instead occur in the violently racist context of American society.
>
> (Lopez 156)

Racial relations in Somerville and in Bianca's family history have led her to assert a specifically non-White identity. She latches onto the *quinceañera* as symbolic of this choice (among many other motivating factors for the celebration of course) and the impact that being a Salvadoran Latina in Somerville has had upon her experiences. Because Jessica, in this same context, would not be viewed as any other race, she does not need to make that same choice as Bianca and distinguish herself from the White population.

Individual differences certainly set Bianca and Jessica apart, however here race proves to be a common feature that influences both their self-perceptions and their understanding of the *quinceañera*. Bianca is often called Blanca (White) as a term of endearment, whereas Jessica's family and friends refer to her as La Negra, a name that emphasizes her dark skin and visibly indigenous roots. Due to her skin tone, Jessica could never pass as anything but Latina—chance granted her darker skin and therefore unquestionable entrance into the Latino community. Bianca, however, wanting similar recognition, exerts power over her racial identity through the choice factor, and deliberately highlights this cultural event as emblematic of her Latinidad. This contrast between Jessica and Bianca is relevant in the way it shows how race plays out in a cultural performance and manipulates its significance. The U.S. groups Latinos under one label as if they constitute a monolithic and uniform population. Clearly, however, all Latinos are not experiencing this label in the same way. While the *quinceañera* is a custom that many Latin/o communities do maintain, the event does not exist in isolation and is shaped by both the community and the honoree's experiences. The honoree is constantly subject to external power systems that leave her raced, classed, and gendered, as all people. These differences manifest themselves in the performance of the *quinceañera* and alter its significance.

One's class is another element of identity that weaves its way into the performance, influencing both the shape of the celebration and its significance to the honoree. Given the *quinceañera*'s propensity towards conspicuous consumption and Somerville's status as a working class city, economic tensions have understandably arisen around the celebration. Each narrator spoke about their perception of spending and the *quinceañera*, a debate to be further explained in the following chapter.

"Tienen padrinos de todo . . ."

ECONOMIC FACTORS IN THE QUINCEAÑERA

For *quinceañera* honorees, the *quinceañera* is like a wedding ". . . only without the groom," many narrators quipped. Girls typically dress in gowns that reach to the ground and cost upwards of $600. The honoree, accompanied by fourteen *damas* (bridesmaids), fourteen *compañantes* (their escorts), and her *chamberlán* (the honoree's date), often rides from the church to her party in a limousine. There, they are professionally photographed, dance to music provided by a DJ or live band, eat a catered meal, and share a three-layer cake for dessert. Nelson Salazar says that such expenses total between five and ten thousand dollars. Norma E. Cantú's study, "La Quinceañera: Towards an Ethnographic Analysis of a Life Cycle," documents similar spending trends in the *quinceañera* through the experiences of several participants from two towns along the Tamaulipas Texas border, Nuevo Laredo and Laredo. "In 1962, we paid no more than $30 for my dress. In the 1990s, a dress can cost anywhere from about $100 to well over $1,000 depending on the embroidery required and the cost of the fabric chosen." Heidy Castro estimates that her family spent four thousand dollars on her *quinceañera* and items like the dress, flowers, cake, party space, photography, DJ, donation to the church, food, and *recuerdos* (mementos). According to the 2000 census, the average per capita income for Hispanics or Latinos in Somerville was $16,490 compared to $25,692 per capita income of its White population (ePodunk 2004). Although few Somerville families have the kind disposable income where they can afford five to ten thousand dollar birthday parties, the coming of age custom continues. While Heidy believes one should set limits on expenditures, she realizes that many families prefer to incur debts rather than have a more modest party for their fifteen year old. Many Somerville Latinos do modify the *quinceañera* to fit their budgets, though others certainly prioritize luxury and, as Heidy pointed out, would rather fall into debt than compromise their custom.

Even residents of Somerville's low-income housing developments have spent exorbitant amounts of money on their daughters' *quinceañeras*. While they may not have the five to ten thousand dollars that Mr. Salazar says many families do spend on the parties, in the past they have rented limousines, bought fancy dresses, and hosted affairs the size and extravagance of a wedding. Mr. Salazar, whose community organization "The Welcome Project" is located amidst one set of Somerville's public housing developments, assures this is true. The poor too, he alleges, have driven themselves into debt for a *quinceañera*; Mr. Salazar reflects on that fact by saying,

> I have a hard time with that. Because it's something that's . . . more like for upper class. For me, that's always been an issue because usually the people that don't have are the ones that tend to imitate. It's kind of sad sometimes to see people who get in debt because they want to have the parties.

He explains that many families may rationalize this spending by looking at the *quinceañera* as the last party they will have for their daughters, the last big event before the wedding. Still, Mr. Salazar believes many others look to the upper class and to each other, constantly trying to affect wealth and to "do it better . . . almost like a competition." In his view, dating back to the European origins of the *quinceañera*, the custom's social component has always facilitated an intentional exhibit of wealth, even when that wealth does not exist; in the context of Somerville, the result is a sad display of the poor emulating the rich. Mr. Salazar's perspective echoes that of bell hooks who states,

> Tragically, the well-off and poor are often united in capitalist culture by their shared obsession with consumption. Often times the poor are more addicted to excess because they are the most vulnerable to all the powerful messages in the media and in our lives in general which suggest that the only way out of class shame is conspicuous consumption.
>
> (hooks 46)

bell hooks exposes the way that capitalism has cultivated a belief that visible consumption signals success. Narrators disagreed, however, on the root of this mentality.

Mr. Salazar believes that Salvadoran tradition does not preclude this same desire to create a spectacle of the *quinceañera*. Remembering those fiestas he attended in El Salvador, Mr. Salazar says the level of excess certainly differed; Salvadorans did not dress in tuxedoes or have limousines to bring them to the church, instead people had to walk. But Mr. Salazar assures, "the big thing about it was that people would see them walking home." The honoree, *chamberlán*, and fourteen *damas* and *compañantes* would parade in what Nelson remembers as a "circus" like fashion to and from the quinceañera. They were well aware and pleased at the idea that the community would emerge to watch the show of it all. Aside from its other social and religious functions, the point of the *quinceañera* was to make others take note of the ceremony's degree of extravagance. Mr. Salazar comments that while Latina *quinceañeras* have undergone certain changes, this is one tradition that has been preserved and finds its roots in Latin America.

Heidy, in contrast, remembers those *quinceañeras* she attended in El Salvador as simpler and attributes their now apparent materialistic quality to United States influence. "En El Salvador yo fui a una quinceañera. Era un pocito más sencilla—no habia tanto lujo como aquí. Pero siempre las quinceañeras son bonitas allí," she said. (In El Salvador I went to a *quinceañera*. It was a little simpler—not such luxury as there is here. But the *quinceañeras* are always nice [in El Salvador].) In fact, she believes that the tendency towards excessive spending has only become more extreme in Somerville; it is a product of younger generations. Heidy remembers her mother being quite resistant when the discussion of hosting a *quinceañera* first arose in the Castro house for this same reason. According to Heidy, her mother initially refused her a *quinceañera*, saying that now one would be too expensive—they are always too extravagant in the United States. Due to her daughter's long-time dream of celebrating her *quinceañera*, Heidy's mother eventually relented.

To explain how some Somerville Latinos manage to maintain this high level of luxury despite economic constraints, Heidy points to the increasing tradition of adopting *padrinos*.[1] The honoree and her family delineate their expected costs for the *fiesta* and then ask others to assume a portion by contributing a specific item. Describing this tradition, Heidy spun off a litany of *padrinos* that one might search for, "que de zapatos, que del anillo, que de vestido, que de limousine, que de pastel, que de local, de música" ([padrinos] of the shoes, the ring, the dress, the limousine, the cake, the salon, the music). Heidy identifies the visible reliance on *padrinos'* contributions as one difference between her own *quinceañera* and more recent ones (in the last six years). She described a greater vanity developing among girls today—a constant desire to be the object of attention by finding more *padrinos* and spending more money. Like Nelson Salazar, Heidy believes there is now a competitive element to the *quinceañera*. The honorees want to exceed what came before them, they want to prove themselves to their peers and to the community.

Heidy did not incorporate sponsors into her *quinceañera*. Her parents bought her the ring (to be blessed by the priest at the religious ceremony) and some aunts and uncles contributed to the *quinceañera* as well, but as their birthday gifts and not as *padrinos*, Heidy distinguishes. She says that her mother insists the *padrino* custom is a burden to others, "Yo no quiero poner cosas en otras personas. *Yo* te traje en este mundo; *yo* te quiero celebrar tus quince años" (I don't want to put responsibilities on others. *I* brought you into this world; *I* want to celebrate your fifteenth birthday). The family refused to turn to relatives and the community for the sake of creating an unnecessarily luxurious event. Still, Heidy knows that most Somerville Latinos "tienen padrinos de todo" (have sponsors for everything). In fact, she says they find so many *padrinos* to assume partial responsibility for the quinceañera that the party is of practically no cost to the family. It should be noted, though, that despite Heidy's assertion, some families do accumulate (and pay) tremendous *quinceañera* bills; of course there would not be cases of debt and bankruptcy if it were not for at least some personal spending.

Community perception of the *padrino* role certainly varies. For instance, Milagro Garcia agrees that families look for *padrinos* so that they spend less on the *quinceañera*, but says that if people want to help financially then that is fine. She also disagrees that sponsorship is a North American ritual, saying that South and Central Americans take part in it as well—she assures, if they can find *padrinos* to contribute, they will.

Heidy argues that asking others to act as sponsors is burdensome and a means of exhibiting vanity without undertaking the extra cost, though there is a dual purpose to this custom. Norma E. Cantú underscores, "The custom of sponsorship mainly serves a twofold function" (Cantú 1999). Beyond deflecting some of the financial burden away from the honoree's family, she says it also "[provides] a social glue for the honoree between her immediate family and the rest of her family and friends" (Cantú 1999). Just as Heidy believes her *quinceañera* exposed her to and expanded her community, Cantú's study reveals that some participants of the *quinceañera* find that asking others to serve as *padrinos* strengthens relationships and serves to honor those on both sides of the relationship. Adopting *padrinos* allows the honoree and her family to more deeply involve the community in this cultural tradition that is the *quinceañera*. Those contributing individuals become wrapped up in what is a milestone in the life of a fifteen-year-old, and a bond is established.[2] Parents are similarly able to interact with the larger community and create or strengthen relationships. Especially in immigrant communities where perhaps the social network is composed of fictive kin rather than extended family, sponsorship can be indicative of a cohesive community. Asking others to financially contribute to the *quinceañera* would lead one to believe that there is a level of trust and shared emotional connection among community members that may not be blood related. Thus the *padrino* custom becomes an adaptive feature among immigrant families in Somerville. In this process of contracting sponsors, then, the *quinceañera* proves its communal, as opposed to just individual, function.

It may also be, that the community is aware of its economic constraints and the fact that, alone, few Somerville families would be able to sustain the *quinceañera* in its traditional form and extravagance. If this is true, then one may interpret the role of *padrinos* as a statement of the community's ability to come together and spend money as a unit. In this light, the system of sponsorship becomes an empowering, rather than degrading custom in the *quinceañera*. Economic tensions, however, remain in Somerville.

According to Norma E. Cantú, "the quinceañera dress marks a change in the wearer's status in the community," (Cantú 1999) in that it signals her transition from girl to *señorita* and availability for marriage. For many honorees in the Somerville Latino community, their perception of the *quinceañera* dress is also an indicator of their feelings related to class. Business owner Milagro Garcia gives insight into this market. Upon immigrating to the United States in 1988, Ms. Garcia opened a boutique that caters to women's *quinceañeras*, weddings, and graduation ceremonies. Her best form of advertisement has been her clientele (composed of Brazilians, Haitians, and Salvadorans), who spread news of the store by word of mouth. Somerville girls, she says, wear conservative dresses—they do not tend to be very extravagant, though they do try to look like princesses, dressed in long gowns, their heads adorned with tiaras. Dresses vary in color depending on the honoree's nationality or ethnicity; for example, the traditional Colombian color is yellow, while the traditional Salvadoran *quinceañera*, referred to as the "fiesta rosa," (rose party) dictates that girls select pink. Rarely would a girl choose a color like red or black for her *quinceañera* dress, however, since the dress is intended to communicate her purity and innocence. Quite often, girls first go online to *quinceañera* websites (of which there are many) or sites of various dress companies. Later they visit Doña Milagro's with a specific image in mind that they hope to find. For those still unsure of what they are looking for, Ms. Garcia keeps catalogues with Latin American, Asian, and American styles—a bit of everything.

Jessica bought her tiara at Doña Milagros, but went to Building Nineteen in Lynn, Massachusetts, for her jewelry, shoes, and dress. Jessica remembers that one friend's dress "was a gown, it looked like she was getting married, honestly." This, however, was not Jessica's goal. She realizes that many families spend more money on *quinceañeras* than she was prepared to on her own,

"I don't think they should go all wild. But at the same time . . . maybe they're, like, you know this is something I want to remember, and this is the way I want to have it. . . . I can't say anything to that." In picking out her own dress, Jessica looked for something more informal that she would be able to wear again. Hers was the traditional pink, a dress that reached to the floor with spaghetti straps and subtle bead embroidery.

Bianca had a similarly modest *quinceañera* and in an untraditional fashion, made all preparations in the weeks leading up to the day (as opposed to months before). She describes the celebration as a "last minute type of a thing," "really simple," and "somewhat elegant." Bianca's godmother offered to buy her *quinceañera* dress as a gift and took her shopping. They went to stores like Bloomingdales, Lord & Taylors, and Filenes, searching for an inexpensive dress, "sort of like a prom dress." She finally selected a lilac colored dress with spaghetti straps from Lord & Taylors. To complete the ensemble, Bianca's aunt styled her hair, braiding the front, and curling the back down to her hips. She wove purple and pink flowers throughout to complement the dress. Bianca emphasized that her dress "wasn't like this big puff wedding dress. It was like somewhat casual but not too casual so I guess it was kind of fancy . . . I've seen fancier but it was fancy." Most girls wear "big puffs for dresses," she mocked, a style that Bianca says she would have been very uncomfortable in, considering her *quinceañera* took place on a hot summer day in July. In retrospect, though, Bianca admits being somewhat regretful that she did not have a classic *quinceañera*, "I kind of wish now that I would have had gone with the pink, would have went traditional." Despite the fact that these traditions do not exist in her family (Bianca's mother did not celebrate her *quinceañera*), the Latino community's traditions are valuable to Bianca. Her continuous emphasis on the difference between her own dress and a traditional one, though, seemed to imply that Bianca's class consciousness also plays into how she looks upon her *quinceañera*.

Bianca, as my student partner, helped to interview Jessica and raised the topic of dress style. "If you could have your *quinceañera* again, and lets say you didn't really have any limits of money, would you do it bigger and poofier, the dress?" she asked. Jessica replied, "It was something special for me, and I wouldn't change it at all." It should be noted though, that despite the way both Jessica and Bianca joked about such dresses, both implied throughout the interview that greater material in the dress indicates greater economic status—the "poofier" and bigger the dress, the more extravagant is was thought to be. For the honoree, the *quinceañera* dress, perhaps more than any other component, is reflective of class playing into the celebration, a performance of wealth.

While the Salvadoran *quinceañera* is closely tied to religion, this apparent materialistic element is at odds with the church's religious agenda. Nelson Salazar recalls having to convince his local priest to say a mass for Bianca. Nelson explains, the priest "doesn't like to do *quinceañeras*," and views their performance as ostentatious. The Salazars connected with the priest on this issue, though, and informed him that theirs would be a modest celebration, at which point he agreed and prepared a traditional ceremony that focused on Bianca's transition from childhood to adulthood. Cantú cites a similar conflict saying, "Mara de la Luz Rodriguez Cárdenas recalls her *quinceañera* of 1960 where the priest refused to say a mass claiming it would be too much like a wedding (personal conversation)." Heidy Castro relates to this moral conflict, though, and says that although the most important quality of a *quinceañera* is the way that it presents a young woman to God, many girls are forgetting, never absorbing, or replacing this religious value with a consumerist one. Still, since the *quinceañera* is not an official sacrament, whether the priest obliges and conducts a religious service is up to his own discretion.

Daisy Gómez, director of C.C.D. at Saint Benedict's, admits that she too was initially reluctant to accept the *quinceañera* as a religious event. Preempting her statements about economic tensions, Ms. Gómez clarified that she is by no means modern, but old school, very traditional, and very much a devout Catholic. Seeing all of the poverty, hunger, homelessness in the world and especially in Latin America, Ms. Gómez could not only not relate to a family that would spend thousands on a *quinceañera*, but she also considered it a sin to do so. She could not understand why such families would not live more humbly and send six of the eight thousand they might spend on a *quinceañera*, to families struggling in Latin America. This was how she viewed *quinceañeras* from the beginning, and in many ways continues to see them. Ms. Gómez could never fathom spending fifteen thousand dollars on a party, and would rather give that money to another—whether she knew that person or not. "Este mundo está lleno de necesidades, no, y va un poco contra nuestra fe también" (This world is full of need, right, and it also goes a bit against our faith), she says of sustaining this materialistic aspect of *quinceañeras*. Catholics are supposed to value and assume poverty—though not misery, she discerns—and to live humbly. While Daisy Gómez, a Cuban American, and the Salvadorans of Saint Benedict's share the Catholic religion, they certainly do not share an understanding of the *quinceañera*. She points out that upon her entrance into the Saint Benedict's community, "En realidad, ellos [los salvadoreños de San Benito] me enseñaron a mi!" (In reality, they [the Salvadorans of Saint Benedict's] taught me!") By interacting with and listening to this community, Daisy Gómez came to a new understanding of the *quinceañera*'s relationship to the church.

She has since watched families, poor families, work multiple jobs to earn enough money to host a *quinceañera* and has witnessed their sacrifice. Mothers want to give their daughters what they never had. This too, Ms. Gómez believes, is valid—"también los pobres sueñan" (the poor also dream). It is perfectly legitimate, she argues, to want for your children what you never had.

Bianca Salazar relates to this concept as she envisions her own daughter's fifteenth birthday celebration, saying she would start saving money for the quinceañera the moment her daughter was born. "I would want something big for her, I want to make it special, have everyone there that she wants and like have it with all the *damas* and the *chamberlán*, and make it that whole big thing cause I wasn't able to do it," she says. Her mother did not have a *quinceañera*, which is why having given her a *quinceañera* at all was a big deal. Bianca assures she enjoyed her own *quinceañera*, though because she had not previously been to one, she hadn't an idea of what a more conventional celebration could look like. With more money spent, her friends have had "prettier" *quinceañeras*, with "more of a party atmosphere," something of which Bianca is certainly jealous. She jokes, "I probably would go to the extreme—whether she liked it or not. I'd be like, 'You're having one!'" Clearly Bianca would like to continue this tradition of giving more to the next generation and understands how this might be a motivating factor for many to indulge in their daughter's *quinceañera*.

Milagro Garcia points to this very idea by saying, every person has their own way of making themselves happy and if it is through hosting a decadent *quinceañera*, then so be it. A mother of two daughters, Ms. Garcia did not give either one a *quinceañera*—there was no question, she could not spend the money. In Ms. Garcia's innumerable interactions with honorees and their families, though, she has noticed that "laz mamás disfrutan a veces más la fiesta que las muchachas" (sometimes the mothers enjoy the parties more than the girls). Since Somerville's Latino population largely stems from a 1980s wave of immigration, many individuals represent the first of their families to have made it to the United States. They have migrated and reestablished themselves and communities, creating a home and a new opportunity out of Somerville. An elaborate *quinceañera*, in this respect, may be symbolic of a family's immigration success and their ability to retain culture despite a new social, political, and economic landscape. Mothers who own this tradition for the first time or moving beyond their own modest *quinceañera* signal to their families and communities, new and old, their enhanced status in a new nation. Moreover, it is a way for parents to connect their child to the home country, to give them that same tangible piece of Latinidad that Bianca says she found in her *quinceañera*.

Families work night and day, but they satisfy the dream. This dream, Ms. Gómez says, first belongs to the parents, who then slowly instill it in their children. She went on to explain by drawing an analogy to a woman who dreams of her wedding day all her life and instills this dream over the years in her child. The girl looks to other role models, sisters, cousins, and brides and a desire for the same wedding grows within her, "como un virus . . . y germina y llega el momento en que tu dices esto es lo que quiero para mi!" (like a virus . . . and it grows and then arrives the moment when you say this is what I want for myself!" A baby is not born with this image of the perfect wedding or *quinceañera*. The first time a girl starts to think about her wedding day, Ms. Gómez believes, is on her first communion—dressed beautifully in white with a crown on her head, it is as if she is a miniature bride. This image is then modified in the *quinceañera*. Once a mother's dream for her daughter, the girl learns to want the same thing, "es un sueño compartido—un sueño que comienza con los padres y lo pasan a los hijos y lo es copartido" (it is a shared dream—a dream that begins with the parents and they pass it to the children and there it is shared). Together, they bring the dream to life.

Bianca, Jessica, and Heidy each collaborated with their families to attain this dream, taking partial financial responsibility for their *quinceañeras*.

Bianca's wages from her summer job enabled her to pay for a professional manicure, a privilege she had never enjoyed before. At first, Jessica was unsure whether she would even have a *quinceañera*. She explains, "It was too expensive and all that stuff. . . . But I started working and with the money that I earned and my mom helped me too, we had the *quinceañera* and I just wanted a simple thing, like something to remember." Aware of the sacrifices a *quinceañera* implies, Jessica decided to work at Mystic Mural, a community beautification project. "For me it wasn't worth it to waste so much money," she says, and decided to have a relatively formal party. Like Jessica and Bianca, Heidy worked to earn money for her family and her *quinceañera*. At age fourteen she began working at a book company making book covers, then at a restaurant at night, and eventually in a pharmacy. These honorees' each played an active role in their celebrations. While they may have compromised their parties due to economic constraints, the contributions they did make allowed each to enjoy a special ownership over their *quinceañeras* that they might not otherwise have had.

Ms. Gómez, with a new understanding of the Salvadoran *quinceañera* and its significance, generally welcomes the celebration at Saint Benedict's. She does, however, take issue with the way that families so quickly forget the church and its needs. The church concentrates on helping old, disabled, vulnerable people and at the same time needs to take care of heating, maintaining the religious school, etc., Ms. Gómez emphasizes. Meanwhile, families want the space to hold a religious ceremony, light, heating, lessons, a priest, and music. They want to spend eight to ten thousand dollars on a party she says—on dresses, limousines, and flowers but are reluctant and resentful when they are asked to contribute two hundred dollars to the church to cover its expenses. She continued to say, every bunch of flowers families have delivered to the church costs between eighty and one hundred dollars, and they often order up to five; they send away for invitations; they send away for dresses. All this, she says, is done painlessly; but when the church asks for a donation of two hundred dollars, that is suddenly too expensive and the family does not have the money. In her view, families should have the consciousness to donate to and take care of the church for all that it contributes to the ceremony. Over the years this is one area in which Ms. Gómez has had to negotiate with the community, though she admits that nowadays families do not protest as they initially did and are much more willing to give.

Despite this stated conflict over excessive spending and financial responsibility for the church's *quinceañera* expenses, Daisy Gómez says that there are instances when the church will sponsor a *quinceañera* itself. When a tradition is healthy, strong, beautiful, and important to the family the church must respect it and accommodate. This is especially true, Ms. Gómez asserts, in cases of extreme poverty, where a family has no means of providing a *quinceañera* or negotiating funds within the community. Then, Daisy Gómez, in conjunction with Saint Benedict's, attempts to compensate for the family's lack of funds. She reflects on one such event, saying, the church made sure the family would be able to have the most beautiful mass and refused to accept any money donation. The choir provided the loveliest music and, Ms. Gómez assures, it was worth it.

"You'll see, San Benito's is like big family."

THE RELIGIOUS COMPONENT OF *QUINCEAÑERAS*

Perhaps the best place to experience this Salvadoran community is through Saint Benedict's church. On a Sunday early in December 2004, I attended an 11:30 AM Spanish mass there with one Tufts student and another Sommerville high school student. The church quickly filled, as hundreds of young Latino children from four to seventeen walked over from Sunday school, just a block away. Along the path between the two buildings, they joined parents, cousins, and siblings, though it was hard to tell who was related to whom. Every one of the hundreds of parishioners seems to know each other. They greet each other with smiles and a kiss on the cheek, a warm handshake. The mass did not start for several minutes. Almost every seat taken, women still paced the aisles, rocking babies until the director called into a microphone that mass would begin. Many toddlers walked freely about the church, their mothers eyeing their movements, though comfortable in this safe community. Teenagers and adults casually picked up wandering children, praised them with glowing smiles, and then passed them to the next person. I watched as my friend Jessica lifted a boy who was no more than two-years-old onto her lap. She must have held him for twenty minutes, kissing his cheek and responding to his inquisitive demeanor by marveling at stained glass or the details of the figures at one Station of the Cross. He went back and forth between the two of them comfortably for the remainder of mass. While the two women had never met, they recognized each other from previous masses and there was an unspoken level of trust they shared. Jessica explained to me, "You'll see, San Benito's is like a big family."

The *quinceañera* is just one shared tradition that has proven to integrate new members into this family and make it stronger. Because of such success, Saint Benedict's Parish has basically institutionalized the ceremony. Bianca explains, "Before you do your confirmation you have to be like sixteen, seventeen. So the *quinceañera* usually happens and that's probably the beginning of your first year or two when you start doing your confirmation." Now considered a mature member of the community, the honoree strengthens her relationship with the church by preparing for her *quinceañera*. Bianca points out that basically every female who attends the Spanish masses at Saint Benedict's has or will have a *quinceañera*. "So it's almost . . . required in a sense, but not necessarily," she says, meaning that if her relationship with the church is to advance, a girl is expected to initiate that growth with her *quinceañera*. While the quinceañera is not a sacrament, the Latino community and Saint Benedict's have found a formal way to integrate the custom into its traditions.

On the day of her *quinceañera*, the honoree stands before a priest and her congregation, ready to enter a new stage of life. The priest blesses her new ring and necklace, and she offers a bouquet of flowers to the Virgin Mary asking for continued guidance and protection. C.C.D. director Daisy Gómez distinguishes the Salvadoran *quinceañera* as "unida muy intimamente con la religión" (tied very closely to religion), more so than the Cuban tradition. The religious mass however, interlaces social values into the *quinceañera*, communicating an honoree's renewed dedication to both Christianity and her community. It grants the honoree space for self-expression, as so many choose to read a poem dedicated to their parents. Usually, she thanks them for the work they have put into the *quinceañera* and the sacrifice that this celebration implies. The mother or father will then often read their own poem dedicated to their daughter, Ms Gómez says, after which the whole family becomes emotional and cries. At Saint Benedict's, the religious component of the *quinceañera* is a mass of thanksgiving, one that communicates values of both piety and community.

Daisy Gómez says that the girls must attend C.C.D. at Saint Benedict's every Sunday from 10:15–11:00 to show that they are committed to Catholicism and that the *quinceañera* does in fact have religious meaning for them. As director of this program, Ms. Gómez and her assistant and Saint Benedict's lecturer, Berta Guevara, hold two *charlas* or informal meetings, one with the honoree and the other in which her family joins. These talks, Ms. Gómez says, are based on "tópicos de actualidad" (everyday topics) such as concepts of respect, morality, the importance of education, what it means to be a good citizen, and the relationship between people and God. The *quinceañera* provides churches the opportunity to "caminar con ellos [las familias], llevarlos de la mano, acompañarlos o que ellos nos lleven a nosotros" (walk with them [the families], take them by the hand, accompany them, or that they carry us). Having institutionalized the *quinceañera*, Saint Benedict's can take advantage of the event by communicating on a more personal level with individuals of the congregation. Berta Guevara uses these *charlas* to talk with youth about the prospects of becoming a nun. She says this is the time when they may realize that God is touching them in a special way, that they have some sort of calling. Sometimes youth just need someone to reassure them of that feeling and offer them the opportunity to become further engaged in the church. Ms. Guevara views the *quinceañera* as that perfect opportunity, and readily finds ways to integrate willing youth into Saint Benedict's. The church's use of the *quinceañera* as a recruitment tool is quite intentional, and at least according to Ms. Guevara and Ms. Gómez, has been a success.

In efforts to further engage youth and ensure their retention in the congregation, Saint Benedict's extends itself beyond the religious and into the social realm of its Latino community. Berta Guevara attempts to relate to the girls through her *charlas* and speaks candidly about the dangers of bad influences, prostitution, and gangs, all of which she claims are very real problems in Somerville. Pointing to visible problems of teen pregnancy in the community, Berta warns youth of the dangers of premarital sex and how being a young mother can affect and change their everyday lives. With hopes of empowering honorees, Ms. Guevara contrasts these negative images with those of youth invested in the church. The *quinceañera* acts as a tool to both ensure the longevity of the congregation and to connect the church with at-risk youth.

Through the *quinceañera* the church also gains access to the honoree's social circle. C.C.D. director, Daisy Gómez, points out that when one invites people to listen to their friend's mass, they often find themselves connected to something greater. Peers engage one another in the religious ceremony in a way that the church cannot. Ms. Gómez acknowledges that many people remember being forced into Christianity as children and because they were too young to appreciate its value, grew distant from the church. Often times these people will return as adults and come to embrace the religion they were born into. The *quinceañera*, Ms. Gómez believes, has many times been a factor in expanding and welcoming Christians back into the religious community. She assures that while one may return specifically for a *quinceañera*, that person will realize what he has lost over the years by distancing himself from the church. Ms. Gómez speculates that God had these same intentions, for the *quinceañera* to give people another opportunity to renew their faith,

De cierta manera es una de los vínculos que establece Dios con la comunidad para que muchas personas que se habían alejado o nunca habían venido. Vuelvan de nuevo y por lo menos o si una vez más, vuelvan a saborear un poco lo que es la fe, la religión, nuestra iglesia.

In a certain way it's a link that God establishes with the community for all of those who have distanced themselves or have never come [to St. Benedict's]. They return again and at least or one more time, they come to savor a bit of faith, religion, and our church.

The quinceañera's social quality allows Saint Benedict's entrance into greater Somerville, facilitating its outreach and effect on the community.

"Es la oportunidad de hablar con los varones, no solamente la hembra."

FIESTAS CLAVEL: A SOMERVILLE-BORN TRADITION

Until 2002, the Somerville *quinceañera* marked a young woman's coming of age and rite of passage into the Christian Latino community. As narrators explain, that year, however, Somerville found a way to extend this ritual to young men of the community. According to Daisy Gómez, in 2002, there was a family who had a fifteen-year-old son that they wanted to present to the congregation during mass. This was not a special *quinceañera* mass but, she continues, the family wanted to thank God and tell him that their son was good. Ms. Gómez goes on to say that while one thanks God daily, the birthday is "un día más marcado," (an especially marked day). Many choose to take advantage of the birthday to thank God and ask that they live one year more.

The following year two twins (a boy and a girl) celebrated their fifteenth birthday and had a joint *quinceañera*. Ms. Gómez said the celebration did not seem too strange since the focus remained on the girl rather than the boy. Later, however, a mother approached Ms. Gómez asking that she help to prepare a *quinceañera* exclusively for her son, for since his birth she had been promising him a *quinceañera*, a ceremony in which she would present him to God and the community. The mother said that it was her son's dream to have a *quinceañera* and requested that Ms. Gómez help arrange the conventional only adapted a bit for a boy. Ms. Gómez admits that though she did not tell the family, she was originally quite skeptical, "Sentí que igual al muchacho lo iba a traumatizar. Sentí que aun la mamá era una de estas mamás que son dominantes. . . . Sentí que igaul el muchacho sería centro de quizás de burla de otros varones, no, uno no sabe" (I felt it might traumatize the boy. I felt that this woman might be one of those domineering mothers. I felt that this boy might be the subject of ridicule among others, you know, one doesn't know). Ms. Gómez said she would have to meet with the boy alone, as she does with all other *quinceañeras*, to interview him and talk about his relationship with God and Saint Benedict's; she especially wanted to get a sense of his feelings and whether his mother was pushing him to have a *quinceañera*. She describes her first meeting with the boy, "un día me lo trajeron, y el muchacho estaba *feliz* con sus quince años—super, super, super feliz, emocionado, y esperando el día de sus quince años para llegar a la iglesia con la mamá, el papá y con los bermanitos, todo el mundo" (one day they brought him to me, and the boy was happy with his fifteenth birthday—super, super super happy, excited, and awaiting his fifteenth birthday so that he could arrive at the church with his mother, father, brothers and sisters, and everyone). So, Ms. Gómez, the church, and the family went about making small adjustments to the *quinceañera* to suit this unique honoree.

Normally one refers to the *quinceañera* as the "fiesta rosa" (rose party) but since this one celebrated a boy, the mother decided to call it "fiesta clavel" (carnation party), finding the latter more masculine. On the day of his *quinceañera*, the boy arrived at Saint Benedict's dressed in a military suit, his family matching its blue color. According to Ms. Gómez, Heidy Castro, and Berta Guevara, the mass turned out beautifully and thus established the fiesta clavel. For the church, the first fiesta clavel was a complete success in the way that it connected Ms. Gómez to this young man. "En realidad me ha resultado tremendamente lindo porque es la oportunidad de hablar con los varones, no solamente la hembra" (In reality it turned out beautifully because it is an opportunity to talk with the males, right, not only females). She had the opportunity to hear what he was thinking, how he saw his life and his future, his relationship with his family, church, with the world. The fiesta clavel, Berta Guevara realizes, is a result of this one boy's enthusiasm over his fifteenth birthday, and a significance it held for him that Saint Benedict's had never witnessed in another boy. This eagerness pleases Ms. Guevara for, just as she had with girls in the past, she could attempt to connect with him on his excitement over a religious event. Ms. Guevara seized this opportunity to talk with the boy about his future in the church, this time encouraging his entrance into priesthood. Although she says the boy might not have genuinely considered the idea at the time, it may be a thought he returns to later in life so the prospect is worth mentioning. In any case, Saint Benedict's believes this boy was special; Ms. Gómez describes him as "limpio," (pure) and "sano," (healthy) making this particular *quinceañera* quite refreshing in this day and age. The church sees potential for him to deepen his relationship with the church, using the fiesta clavel as a jumping off point for further investment.

The three fiestas clavel that Saint Benedict's has had have all been much more modest presentations than those of young women. Ms. Gómez guesses that the boys are more timid than the girls, and says that just because they have a *quinceañera* does not mean that they stop being men. "De todas maneras, las mujeres son mucho más escandolosas que los hombres" (In every way the women are much more scandalous than the men), she joked. While the boys attend the religious ceremonies and behave themselves extremely well throughout their fiestas clavel, "no andan con la pompa y el brillo de la hembra" (they don't go around with the same pomp and brilliance as the girl). In their revised form, Ms. Gómez assures that the fiesta clavel will become a popular tradition. In fact, Ms. Gómez recently spoke to a priest friend of hers at another church telling him about the fiesta clavel. Elated at the idea of a fiesta clavel, the priest assured that he would adopt it in his church, liking the idea so much because the soul has no sex and all individuals should be able to present their souls to God. Ms. Gómez agrees there is no reason for the woman to always be the one that is wrapped up in religion while the man remains detached. Through the fiesta clavel, Ms. Gómez explains, the man declares that he too is the son of God, wants to have a relationship with God, and that he eventually wants to create a family with a religious base. Heaven, she assures, is open to all that have faith in whatever God and religion they choose, as long as it is a healthy one. Therefore, it is important that men find a way to establish this kind of relationship with God as well, and if the *quinceañera* helps this process, then the tradition should certainly continue.

Heidy Castro believes that the *quinceañera* will in fact catch on in the community, remembering how her own brother wished to have one when he was a child. A younger sibling, Heidy's brother could not understand why she was so celebrated and that he would not be, or at least never in so formal a manner. Noting their son's genuine longing for a *quinceañera*, Heidy's parents started planning a smaller party for him. When his fifteenth birthday came, however, her brother changed his mind. Since his fifteenth birthday preceded the birth of the fiesta clavel, he worried that others would think him strange, echoing similar preoccupations as Daisy Gómez initially expressed. Heidy assures, however, that community has received those boys who have had *quinceañeras* very well and without ridicule. If her brother were just turning fifteen now, she is fairly confidant that he would want a *quinceañera* and that this history of fiestas clavel would make him less insecure. Boys, she believes, are looking for a connection to the church and something to mark their growth as members of society too. The fiesta clavel encourages that men similarly engage and invest in the community. It provides an opportunity for Saint Benedict's to show its appreciation of their commitment to Christianity and to create a relationship that the church hopes will develop into a long-lasting and mutually beneficial connection. Unclear whether this tradition is sprouting in other communities, the fiesta clavel may be Somerville's most marked contribution to the *quinceañera* tradition. It is a source of pride for the community and further encouragement that the church has and will continue to impact the lives of young people.

FINAL REMARKS

A study on the *quinceañera* in Somerville shows how one tradition that is present across Latin American and Latino communities as a coming of age ceremony can take on the values of those who practice it. Each of the seven narrators, involved in the *quinceañera* as honoree, participant, provider, or religious leader have influenced the shape of this ritual and adapted it to their own needs. The *quinceañera* has proved itself a link to sending nations, between generations, and for outsiders, a point of entry into understanding Somerville. As an anthropology student, I have been enlightened listening to the stories of these various hospitable, gracious, and candid community members and truly learned the value of documenting oral history. Through one cultural ceremony, I have come to better understand race relations, local politics, class issues, gender identity, and connections between communities in Somerville. The final product, the compiled stories of seven individuals, is emblematic of this population's ability to adapt to new environments while retaining its identity.

As it is celebrated, the *quinceañera* really reflects Somerville's living history and over time will show the growth of this community in itself, but also in relation to the greater socio-cultural landscape. Somerville Latinos are part of a relatively new immigrant community and their cultural practices will continue to adapt and grow with the population. The following topics are those that I could not sufficiently address in the constraints of this semester-long project and would make interesting areas of future study.

1. Bicultural influences in the *quinceañera*. I entered into this project anticipating a more visible influence from dominant U.S. populations on the *quinceañera*. Besides brief comments about changing music in the social celebration (i.e. a stronger presence of reggaetón) and Jessica's bilingual mass, narrators stressed the similarity between Somerville *quinceañeras* and those in Latin America. They all have deep connections to their sending nations and so the Somerville *quinceañera* does not symbolize one reaching back to her roots, for they are so connected to daily life. As Salvadorans establish deeper roots in Somerville, I hypothesize that they will find bicultural influences to be more salient, and perhaps even incorporate the Anglo-American population into these celebrations.

2. Sexuality in the *quinceañera*. I did not delve deeply into this topic during interviews. I felt that as a Tufts University student disconnected from the Somerville Latino population, it might be inappropriate or invasive for me to ask about the girls' sexual experiences. It took me about a month to really learn about the *quinceañera* as it exists in Somerville; to get to know the community; and to understand how and in what context people discuss the

quinceañera. I was reluctant to introduce a topic that could be perceived as taboo when I was so briefly entering the community. However there is surely a wealth of information in this subject area. Some preliminary questions I would suggest are:

    a. How does the church and community regard honorees who are not virgins?

    b. Has having premarital sex kept many girls from having a *quinceañera* in Somerville?

    c. How do parents communicate values around sexuality in the context of the *quinceañera*?

    d. Who makes the rules about quinceañeras and an honoree's sexual activity—is it the church, family, peer group, or greater Somerville?

3. The fiesta clavel. A later study would examine whether the fiesta clavel has indeed become a trend in Somerville; how peer groups perceive the celebration; and what values are distinctly communicated to males in Somerville.

ACKNOWLEDGMENTS

I greatly appreciate the following individuals for so generously and candidly contributing to this project: Heady Castro, Bianca Salazar, Milagro Garcia, Nelson Salazar, Daisy Gómez, Jessica Tejada, and Berta Guevara.

Many thanks also to Professor Pacini-Hernández, Michelle Fuentes, The Welcome Project, Cecilia Dos Santos, Lexie McGovern, Alex Weissman, my mother, Jane Arcaya, St. Benedict's Parish, and the 2004 Urban Borderlands class!

NOTES

1. While *padrinos* literally means godparents in Spanish (*padrino* for godfather and *madrina* for godmother) the term refers to sponsors in the context of *quinceañeras*.

2. *La Quinceañera: Towards an Ethnographic Analysis of a Life Cycle Ritual* purports that the custom of *padrinos* likewise renews old bonds, as many baptisms also incorporate *padrinos*.

REFERENCES

Borgos, Ricardo and Marcuss, Mammie. "Who Are New England's Immigrants?" Accessed on December 13, 2004 at http://www.bos.frb.org/commdev/c&b/2004/Fall/Immigrants.pdf.

Cantú, Norma E. "Chicana Life-Cycle Rituals," *Chicana Traditions: Continuity and Change*, ed. Norma E. Cantú and Olga Najera-Ramirez. University of Illinois Press, 2002. Accessed on December 13, 2004 at http://adelantesterling.tripod.com/quincena_meaning.htm.

Cantú, Norma E. "La Quinceañera: Towards an Ethnographic Analysis of A Life-Cycle Ritual." *Southern Folklore* 56, no. 1 (1999). Retrieved December 03, 2004 at http://colfa.utsa.edu/cantu/quinceahera.html.

"ePodunk: The Power of Place." ePodunk.inc, 2004. Accessed December 2004 at http://www.epodunk.com/cgi-binlincomeOverview.php?locIndex=3133.

hooks, bell. 2000. *Where we stand: Class Matters.* New York: Routledge.

Lopez, Ian F. Hany. 2001. "The Mean Streets of Social Race." The Social Construction of Race and Ethnicity in the United States. Ed. Joan Ferrante and Prince Brown Jr. New Jersey: Prentice Hall.

INTERVIEWS

Arcaya, Sara. Interview with Heidy Castro. Rec. 29 November 2004. Audiotape.

Arcaya, Sara. Interview with Milagro Garcia. Rec. 11 November 2004. Audiotape.

Arcaya, Sara. Interview with Daisy Gomez. Rec. 23 November 2004. Audiotape.

Arcaya, Sara and Salazar, Bianca. Interview with Berta Guevara. Rec. 05 December 2004. Audiotape.

Arcaya, Sara. Interview with Bianca Salazar. Rec. 15 October 2004. Audiotape.

Arcaya, Sara and Salazar, Bianca. Interview with Jessica Tejada. Rec. 15 October 2004. Audiotape.

PART II
TESTIMONIOS

Give Us This Day

Judith Ortiz-Cofer

Había una vez, a girl, a *quinceañera*, who one night learns the power of fear, of *el terror*. Her father has fallen or jumped from the roof of *un edificio*. Not the building where her family lives, but another, in a street of strangers. What was he doing there? No one explains to *la muchacha*. She is, as always, simply summoned to translate. Now she has to walk alone down dangerous streets to get to the hospital. Her mother is already there. And Mother needs words in English. The doctor does not understand her anguish, her *lagrimas*, or her prayers *en español*. En *el hospital* they only speak in questions: Insurance? Do you? Don't you? *Preguntas, de seguro.* Her father *habla ingles*, but he is wrapped in bandages and *en el silencio*. She is afraid of his angry *silencios* at home. Her mother *no habla ingles*, and her father, *silenciado* by a false or true step from the roof of a building where no one he knows lives, lies broken and silent on a hospital bed. It is dark and cold and the streets son *muy peligrosas*. She has never been allowed to *caminar sola*, even in daytime, past these alleys where *el crimen* hides behind a pile of trash, and danger sounds like a starved cat, or like *una pareja* of lovers struggling behind a dumpster. Sounds of *el amor* or *de violencia?* Men huddle under a light post, watching her with their *ojos de muertos*. As she nears them, they fall silent and stare. *Drogaditos. Asesinos. Vecinos.* Friends or foes? *¿Quien sabe?* It is the hour of *el suicidio*, of the casual attack, of the rape, *del asesinato*—the hour of *de murder-me-solo-porque-puedes*, of hurt-me-because-you-can. *El miedo.* The evil hour. She thinks of her father stepping off the roof of *un edificio* where no one he knows lives. She tries to imagine the sound of his body breaking on the pavement. Was he silent? She cannot imagine his voice of pain. But she hears *la voz angustiada* of her mother on the telephone, summoning her into the night at this *mala hora*, for her English. The girl prays, protect me *dolor de mi alma*, make me strong, as she approaches the ones who wait to hurt her, or not. She walks past them wearing her *cara de loca*, a face that tells them she will not serve them as a *victima*, not this *noche*, for she is shielded by a pain-to-come greater than they can inflict on her, with their evil eyes and stranglers' hands. They take a step back into the dark when

Judith Ortiz-Cofer *"Give Us this Day,"* first published in *North American Review*, May–August 2008, vol. 293, no. 3–4:59

she confronts them with her avenging angel eyes, her *cara de loca* face. *Miedo, terror.* She wills them to feel it. The power she has conjured out of her own fear is a fire in her heart that lights her way through *la noche oscura*. This night she is invulnerable. She cannot be assaulted, raped, or killed, for she must get to the hospital to speak Salvation English for her parents. She possesses *el santo ingles*, and she carries it like a gun, like a chalice. She is wears it like a hairshirt, like a bulletproof vest. *Father in Heaven, give us this day our daily English.* She feels powerful as *una santa*, as *una asesina*. Anyone who sees her knows nothing can touch her. Fear and anger propel her through the dark. She must get there to translate her mother's *angustia*, and to help name her father's pain.

La Bendición

Julia Alvarez

Spending a year trying to understand a tradition focused on young Latina teens, I often felt like an adolescent myself, subject to the swings of contradictory feelings about the subject of my study.

But never about the subjects. This I want to make clear. Over and over what I felt toward the girls themselves was a tenderness and protectiveness that surprised me. I had just met many of them. I was not their mother or grandmother or godmother or aunt. But their youth and their vulnerability, their hopefulness and their beauty, touched something womanly and profound in me that—for lack of a better name—could be called the maternal instinct.

Driving home from their *quinceañeras* or hanging up the phone after our interviews, I wanted to continue at their side, accompanying them, advising them, and protecting them, but mostly listening to them, cheering them on. Those feelings, I came to realize, are what coming-of-age ceremonies are meant to ritualize and affirm in a community over time. Somehow, as a nation we've dropped the ball in this regard, leaving our young girls in the lurch, as Mary Pipher warned more than a dozen years ago in *Reviving Ophelia*. Perhaps our leaving them on their own was based on a well-meaning desire to let our young girls experience the freedom and autonomy we ourselves had not been allowed at their age. Many of us, Latina women, especially, grew up with so many prohibitions and inhibitions. Of course, we want our young girls to be free, free, free at last of all the bonds that hobbled and divided us!

But by celebrating their *quinceañeras* these Latina girls are letting us know that they want something more than freedom. They yearn to connect with their history. "It's like part of my Hispanic culture," many responded when I asked them to tell me about this tradition. I appreciated the "like" in their descriptions because it signaled that this tradition is being transformed even as it is being codified by their descriptions.

The *quinceañera* as practiced today in the United States is like a ritual that came from the native countries of grandparents or parents, countries many of these young girls have never been to. But through this tradition, they are reaching back to that old culture, out of a need for community and meaning,

Julia Alvarez: *"La Bendición,"* first published in *Once Upon a Quinceañera: Coming of Age in the U.S.* New York: Viking, 2007.

continuity and direction. A way not to get lost. A way to be and belong: a Latina girl stringing her bead of self in the necklace of the generations.

Not all of us older Latinos and Latinas are first-generation Americans, but *all* of us are the first Hispanics, a group created in 1973 by a stroke of the pen. It is important that we not let another stroke of the pen, metaphorically speaking, define our traditions for us. By this I mean the danger of a runaway consumer culture re-creating and distorting our traditions in order to sell us something. Change is necessary but it should be change based on the needs of our young people, not a corporation's bottom line. Neither should we allow ourselves to be circumscribed by a sacred-cow mentality about native country traditions just because "they are one of the few traditions we have left." Traditions are made of sturdier stuff, and our ongoing responsibility is to revise and renew them so that they continue to fulfill their authentic purpose, to empower us.

Which is why this journey into the world of *quinceañeras* proved to be richer and more complex than I initially suspected. I come out of this year feeling a deeper understanding of the challenges facing our Latino community as we come of age in the United States as well as the challenges facing our daughters and granddaughters as they come of age as young women. We need to be there with them at this important passage, *profundizando* and deepening their sense of what this journey entails. In order to educate them, we have to educate ourselves, as Plato reminds us, about who we are as a community and as new Latina Americans.

This book has been an attempt to do that through the lens of one tradition, the *quinceañera*: to review and understand this evolving ritual with all its contradictions, demystifying its ideology, dusting off the glitter that is sprayed over the ritual in order to be sold back to us by an aggressive consumer market as the genuine article, handing it down in as clear and conscionable a form as possible. My hope is that from the vantage point of this ritual we can begin to understand both our personal past and our collective present, as well as our evolving future as a diverse community within an ever more Latinized nation.

But the swings, dear reader, the swings in my feelings toward the tradition were downright dizzying and baffling. Did I believe in this Q-tradition or not? Yes and no. Sí y no. Back and forth. At dinner parties, I'd relate the details of some Q-extravaganza I'd just been to or heard or read about, and as my friends shook their heads and compared *quinceañeras* to the runaway Bar and Bat Mitzvah parties, I'd find myself backtracking, wanting to defend *nuestra tradición*. "On the other hand," I'd tell my friends.

On the one hand: *quinceañeras* are expensive, especially as they are evolving in our U.S. consumer culture. It is outrageous to throw the house out the window for a one-night party. Money that could well be spent by a working-class family on education or mortgage payments. Then there's the whole issue of a ceremony that encourages young girls in the dubious fantasy of being a princess, a fantasy most of our young girls cannot afford to indulge in. In fact, to revisit Ana Maria's vision under a tree in Memorial Park in Caldwell,

Idaho, the percentages are telling us an altogether different story about what lies ahead for our young people. How can we let ourselves be conned into thinking a hyped-up, supersized production has anything to do with an authentic tradition that can empower our young girls as they become women?

On the other hand: there were times as I sat in a kitchen, watching the women in the family, the mother and grandmothers, the tías and madrinas, making the recuerdos while the court of fifteen young couples practiced their choreographed dances in the living room or backyard, periodically dropping into the kitchen for a snack and to listen to the old stories that inevitably arise when women gather together—those times, I'd feel a special transmission going on. I was a part of something timeless, hard to name or contain. "Something was growing inside of me," says Estrella as her special night approaches in *Estrella's Quinceañera*, "A feeling I hadn't had in a long time. I was part of something bigger. I truly belonged." In that kitchen, I, too, felt a part of a rare and true experience, one I had mostly missed in my own growing up. "We need symbolic action to draw us together and keep us going," Norine Dresser writes in *Multicultural Celebrations*. "That's what these life-cycle celebrations do. They make us feel that we belong. This feeling comes through the creation of *communitas*—a feeling of oneness. . . . Life-cycle celebrations furnish creative outlets for the human spirit . . . confirm spirituality and authenticate life."

That oneness, that empowering feeling of being a part of an ongoing transmission, is what the tradition ritualizes, why quinceañeras are not just about the girls but about community, why they can enrich all of us.

In wanting to hand down a tradition that truly empowers young women, I, of course, worried about the charge of sexism. As traditionally practiced, the *quinceañera* enacts and, therefore, subliminally affirms a patriarchal paradigm, the sexuality of the young girl controlled and monitored by a macho culture. How can any woman who calls herself a feminist want to pass on such a ritual to her daughter?

Over the course of the past year of attending them and immersing myself in their lore, relishing the new, liberated variations, I thought a lot about this charge against quinceañeras. Was it a sign of my own corrupted feminism that I felt the hypnotic pull of this ritual?

What I came to understand about myself and most of the women and girls I interviewed is that there is a hunger in us for this kind of ritual expression that truly respects and honors our female sexuality. In her wonderful essay "Brideland," Naomi Wolf describes experiencing similar baffled feelings as a young feminist preparing for her wedding, a ceremony "that leaves no doubt as to the naked patriarchialism of . . . its origins." In fact, Naomi Wolf feels herself lulled and deeply attracted to this bridal world. Why would a young feminist want to submerge herself in this world of "Brideland"? she asks herself.

> The reason has to do with the modern era's denigration of female sexuality. We live in an age in which female sexuality is held incredibly cheaply; it is on tap; you can gain access to it at the flick of a switch. While few people want the bad

old days of enforced virginity to return, I think there is a terrible spiritual and emotional longing among them for social behavior or ritual that respects, even worships, female sexuality and reproductive potential. We are no longer Goddesses or Queens of our own sexuality.

Paradoxically, swaddled in the white satin of the formal bridal gown, we take on for a moment that lost sexual regalness. . . . We are made into treasure again, and jewels adorn our breasts. In white, we retrieve our virginity, which means metaphorically, the original specialness of sexual access to us. . . .

Who wouldn't want to drift in those currents for a while. . . .

The *quinceañera* offers a young Latina the opportunity to drift in these currents as well, and not because she is marrying someone. This is precisely what Isabella Martínez Wall meant by wanting each girl to feel like a queen of her own life. Of course, none of us older Latinas and feminists would want to go back to the "bad old days," when our rights were curtailed and our hearts and minds divided by either/ors, as my own long and rocky passage to adulthood attests to. But as Wolf concludes, "perhaps the knowledge that we have lost the sense of the value of female sexuality . . . will lead us to find new rituals, new experiences, new ceremonies in which we can announce to the world that we are sexually priceless—and not just for one expensive day."

The *quinceañera* is just such a ritual, but it needs revamping, as I can affirm after a year of feeling as if I were drowning in pink clichés and watching working-class parents dish out dollars "to show off rather than show off their daughters," a distinction a guest made to me about one such party. As the generation passing on the tradition, we need to divest it of its entrapments while at the same time recognizing that beneath them lies a living spring. Mimi Doll, one of the researchers involved with the SHERO project mentioned earlier, made a wonderful observation about tradition. Hearing me grumble about traditions that entrap us and prevent us from full flowering— it was one of my days of swinging into Q-con territory—Mimi Doll reminded me: "Our traditions are meant to take care of us and protect us as a people. So we can't just dismiss them. The challenge is to ensure that we recast them to our present-day context so that they continue to take care of us."

Mimi Doll went on to cite the example of Marianismo, that ideal of Latina womanhood with its heavy emphasis on virginity. The girls in her SHERO project had identified it as one of the powerful behavioral forces in their lives. How can this old paradigm be useful now? "Originally, Marianismo was all about chastity as a sign of the purity of the female and the honor of the family. Our SHERO girls are now talking about chastity in order to protect themselves, so they don't get pregnant, so they can finish high school and go to college."

Our young Latinas should feel free to reimagine the old stories so that they do not feel divided by their dual cultures, as many in my generation did, so that they feel our blessing on their particular expression of their traditions, as many of us did not, to our detriment.

This expansive attitude toward our inherited cultures is, in fact, being embraced by young feminists today. In her introduction to *To Be Real: Tell-*

ing the Truth and Changing the Face of Feminism, Rebecca Walker explains why many young feminists have rejected an earlier generations feminist label: "For many of us to be a feminist in the way we have seen or understood feminism is to conform to an identity and way of living that doesn't allow for individuality, complexity, or less than perfect personal histories. *Third wavers,* as these young feminists call themselves, are "broadening our view of who and what constitutes 'the feminist community,' staking out an inclusive terrain from which to actively seek the goals of Social equality and individual freedom we all share. We are accepting contradiction and ambiguity . . . using *and* much more than *either/or.*"

In our first and second waves of feminism as well as in our first and second generations as immigrants and as newly minted Latinos, we sometimes trap ourselves in too-rigid definitions of what it means to be who we are. As Rebecca Walker reminds us: "The complex, multi-issue nature of our lives, the instinct not to categorize and shut oneself off from others, and the enormous contradictions we embody are all fodder for making new theories of living and relating." So, yes, Rebecca Walker assures her young fellow feminists, you can be a feminist and shave your legs, get married, want to raise three kids on a farm in Montana, still speak to the father who abused you.

How these young feminists are redefining and enlarging the ground of feminism is applicable to our young Latinas as they negotiate and expand the ground of their ethnicity. The very hybridity they inherit because of their dual cultures in addition to the global culture in which they are coming of age means that the traditions we pass on to them have to take into account a more complex and multifaceted and contradictory young person than we ever were at their age. And the *quinceañera* offers them an opportunity to explore that variety and contradiction within the supportive context of family and community, of custom and ceremony. As W. B. Yeats reminds us in his poem "A Prayer for My Daughter," traditions are a society's way of cultivating, protecting, and passing on the things that are important to the new generations:

> How but in custom and in ceremony
> Are innocence and beauty born?
> Ceremony's a name for the rich horn,
> And custom for the spreading laurel tree.

Perhaps out of the same impulse that led me to rouse up some wise women at Andover and construct a ritual that might empower my special girls, I decided to end this book with a gathering of wise women.

I would invite fifteen *mujeres sin pelo en la lengua* to join a court of wise women, truthsayers. I envisioned a kind of virtual *quinceañera* for my readers, who would encounter these *madrinas* here at the close of this book, each one proffering a *consejo,* or piece of advice, that might prove useful to them in the future.

One morning, listening to National Public Radio, I felt affirmed in my decision by a report about a group of elders who dispense advice online. Elder

Wisdom Circle was founded by a forty-four-year-old "youngster," Doug Meckelson, who felt there was a need for guidance among the young and not so young as well as a fund of untapped wisdom in our elders. At the time of the report, Elder Circle was up to 250 volunteers, spread all over the United States, representing eighteen thousand years of experience! (I was tickled by the response to one letter from a thirteen-year-old girl, worried about her older sister's drinking, which began, "Hi, Thirteen Ladies and four gentlemen are responding.")

One of the not so surprising revelations was that the majority of letters seeking advice come from teens. A lot of them write in saying, "nobody listens to me," Sharon Morrison, a member of the circle, told the NPR reporter. Then, musing over why, she sighed. "When you're young you need an authority of age to you find your way."

"It used to be that how we learned was based on dealing with people who had already experienced something," Doug Meckelson elaborated. In fact, his immediate inspiration for founding the circle was his late grandmother, "who gave me advice on everything." But now, as Will Cain, the founder of *Quince Girl*, reminded me about the *quinceañera*, "*La abuelita* is not always a resource." Emigration from our native countries and mobility within this country have forced us to seek advice and knowledge elsewhere, online from Elder Wisdom Circle and from manuals and books like this one.

All the more reason to gather some of those *abuelitas* and wise women here and ask them what piece of advice they would give a young or not so young person who might feel the need for wisdom in today's world.

And so, I began making a list of wise women I knew. The plan was to send out a first round of letters to a handful and wait for a response before sending out a second round. After all, I didn't want to invite too many wise women into the circle and then in the interest of keeping to the thematic number fifteen—boot anyone out. But how to decide? There were so many. The only way to make any kind of a selection was to remind myself that each woman in my circle was representing a heck of a lot of absent ones. A representative congress, more than an oligarchic coven.

Some of the wise women on my list were figures who served a guiding role in my own life: Zanda Merrill and Ruth Stevenson and Cherríe Moraga and Maxine Hong Kingston. Others were figures who serve leadership and inspirational roles in our Latino community or in the larger culture: women like Isabel Allende and Dolores Huerta, the female face of United Farm Workers, and Mary Pipher, author of *Reviving Ophelia*. Some were fellow journeyers like Sandra Cisneros and Norma Cantú and María Hinojosa.

"I am writing you because you are one of the wise women in my life," I explained in my letter. "We are now the elders of the tribe, and as the Hopi elders reminded their tribe during a difficult time, 'We are the ones we have been waiting for.' What can we pass on to our young people as they come of age in today's world? I'd like you to consider that question and join my sacred circle."

"Let me think about it," Ruth Stevenson graciously wrote back. In a later e-mail she admitted, "I'm usually suspicious when I hear the word 'should.'" She did try a couple of times, but what she sent back were not nuggets of wisdom but stories of times when as a young woman she felt the winged life stirring inside her. I had to smile. Of course, my English teacher would tell stories! She knew, as did the Sufi masters, that the best "answer" to give a student is to tell her a story that allows for multiple interpretations and from which she can garner wisdom commensurate with her ability to absorb and understand.

I began to wonder if my great idea was a truly useful way to close this book. But then some "answers" started to trickle in, often prefaced by "Oh my god, only *one* piece of advice?" Or conversely, "Oh my god, I don't know if I believe in *any* advice." Still, many of these big-hearted *mujeres* indulged me and went on to offer what did seem to me very wise advice. But what I realized as I culled these responses and began to draft a second round of letters was that when I was fifteen, what I would have found most useful was not a piece of advice, no matter how wise, but a relationship with the person who was modeling that wise advice in the way she was living her life. Someone who might have listened to me and helped me access the strength and wisdom in myself and apply it to the particular challenges I was facing at that stage of my own life.

Perhaps not surprisingly, the advice I got even from such a varied group of women fell along the same lines. The strongest emphasis was about realizing the power in you. It would seem that in the pantheon of my three little Papo dolls—princess, fairy godmother, woman warrior—the key figure among my wise women is the woman warrior. "Learn your strength," María Hinojosa wrote. "Eat your fear and self-doubt for breakfast!" Isabel Allende agreed. "Take risks," she advised, "because a life without risks is no life at all."

"Don't forget your powers," Zanda Merrill echoed, and went onto list them. Wishing power, staying power, going power, healing power, power to make a change in the world.

During a face-to-face interview in my hotel room in Los Angeles on the eve of a big immigrant march she would be leading, Dolores Huerta responded to my query for advice with a question. Who did I think was the more fierce of a species in the animal kingdom, the male or female?

I could guess the right answer, but I wanted to give her the pleasure of enlightening me. "The male?"

As expected, Dolores answered gleefully, "No! It's the female!"

"That's why I tell young girls, you have to stand up for yourself. Be bien preparadas. If you can't fight for yourself, how can you fight for your family, your community, your country?" It seemed odd to hear such a battle cry from a petite, very pretty seventy-six-year-old woman, dressed daintily in a black pantsuit with a flowered blouse. But her blue black eyes were wise, the eyes of an old soul with a young heart. The beaded necklace ("made for me by a prisoner") with the eagle (*águila*) logo of the United Farm Workers was also a reminder of the long, hard struggles she has fought and continues fighting.

The other major emphasis in the advice received from this first round of my wise women involved finding your magic: the fairy godmother figure in my trinity of dolls. "Use your talents," Norma Cantú advised, and then went on to use hers by proffering fourteen other *consejos*, from the high-minded (set goals, take risks, forgive) to the mundane (exercise, be on time, keep a diary). When

I asked her to pick just one, she went back to "celebrate your gift and share it." Sharing was a key component of Cherríe Moraga's conversation with me. "Remember you live in community. You have a responsibility to be account-able to your family and your community as well as yourself." Cherríe laughed, explaining, she had lost her mother in the summer at ninety years old. "And although I was a rebel, I find my mother's words coming out of my mouth."

Finally, some of the advice was addressed specifically to the princess in our young girls—the last one of my Papo dolls. "Don't become drunk when a pretty (or famous) man pays attention to you," Sandra Cisneros wrote. "Pretty (or famous) men who come after you like gangbusters come after ALL women that way. If I had known that then, I wouldn't have been so naive to think I was selected among all women and honored by their attentions. I thought I had incited them to 'love,' but for men I was simply another four-letter word, which, to be kind here, I'll call 'lust.'"

"No te dejes," Cherríe Moraga echoed. "Don't abandon yourself. If you find yourself in a place where you've betrayed yourself; get out!" Again, Cherríe laughed. Something else her mami used to tell her.

Perhaps because Cherríe kept bringing up her mother, I felt a yearning to call my own mami and find out what she would advise.

I had not intended to ask her to join my circle of wise *viejitas*.

Like most daughters, I felt I had had enough maternal advice to last me all my life, thank you very much. Then, too, Mami and I had had such a rocky relationship since the very years I was writing about in this book on *quincea-ñeras*. Not to mention that in the past she had taken issue with some of my autobiographical writings. She did not buy my defense that my novels were fiction, that I had used what I knew in the service of story, not as a tell-all tabloid would. Beyond the veil of fabrication, she saw the shadowy shape of our own family, our struggles, our failures, and what she refused to see in her rage, our triumphs.

During the height of her hurt feelings toward me, she had been hospital-ized following an ankle fracture, and I had hurried down to New York City to be at her side. My distress and unwavering allegiance—despite my "disobedi-ence"—were reminders that this woman was part of my heart's core, not an appendage I could remove and continue living without.

After visiting her in the hospital, I stayed overnight in the small apartment my parents had moved to in Manhattan after they sold the house in Queens. I slept in her bed, next to Papi's bed. On the small tray on her bedside table was a small jar of Vicks and a tube of face cream, just as on my own bedside table back in Vermont. Below the drawer in a cubbyhole, I found a copy of my first novel, which came as a surprise since I knew my mother had banned my fiction from her home.

I opened it, and what a sick and pained feeling! She had gone through the whole novel highlighting certain passages—some pages literally glowed. Their offensiveness seemed to stem from the mention of sex or drugs or men-tal illness or flawed mothers. I closed the book and stroked the cover—my first novel, my grand achievement that I had hoped would reclaim my stand-ing in the family—and set it back in the cubbyhole where I had found it.

Fifteen years later, to be serendipitously exact, I was going to contact her about being in a book with no pretense that this was fiction! No, I am not a masochist. As it happens, we had found each other again in the last few years. My mother had asked my husband, an ophthalmologist, to remove her cataracts, and she had come up to Vermont and stayed with us during the two procedures. She was grateful to me for welcoming her into my home, to him for "giving me back my sight." Afterward, it was as if her vision—as well as mine—had been figuratively cleared. I heard a new tone in her voice. *My dove, my little one, my child, my daughter.* Meanwhile, I picked up an old-country habit that my sisters and I had discarded over the years. In saying good-bye to our parents, in person or by phone, we would ask for their blessing, "La bendición, Mami, Papi."

"Que Dios to bendiga, mi'ja."

But it was not just nostalgia that was the impulse for my wanting to call my mother and ask for her *consejo* for ending this book. In fact, there had been a sea change not just in our relationship but in our family's story. After forty-two years in this country, she and Papi had moved back to their home-town of Santiago. Soon after the move, my father began the long good-bye, descending into Alzheimer's, forgetting whether or not he had eaten supper or if beyond the windows lay New York City or Santiago, the now very urban, bustling city of his birth, the city where he had chosen to die.

In this most difficult transition, my mother's uncomplaining and tender care of my father, her resilience and joy in life have amazed and impressed her four daughters. It turns out we had underestimated Mami's capacity to handle adversity, to take the lemons life gives you and, as she would have said in her malapropping, mixed-metaphor English, find the silver lining in them.

Hacer de tripas corazón.

But we can sense she is lonely. The calls come more often; she welcomes our visits as she never did in the past when we would arrive from board-ing school or college or our own lives with our noise and demands and our messy ways and our worrisome stories. She has also become an avid baseball fan, rooting for the teams with the most Dominican players, watch-ing the games on cable TV. My mother, who couldn't sit still for a long talk because she always had to be moving. Talking made her nervous, especially talking with her daughters, who had so many strange ideas. Most especially talking with this daughter with her divorces and problematic autobiograph-ical novels.

We are tentative with each other. Our conversation stays within the safe confines of her health and Papi's condition, as if we're still unsure how far afield to wander from our newfound closeness. Sometimes she asks about my writing. When I told her I was working on a *quinceañera* book, she lined up a bunch of great-nieces for me to interview during one of my visits to Santiago and threw a "tea" for all the "girls" who had been presented with me back in the summer of 1967.

So, I was both encouraged but a little nervous to ask her to join my circle of wise women. What would she offer as a *consejo* to a young girl today, a girl who would inevitably wear my teenage face in her imagination?

I sent her an e-mail suggesting the idea to her. A few days later, when I hadn't heard from her, I followed it up with a call.

She was watching a baseball game, the Red Sox against Cleveland—the TV blared in the background—and eating saltines, a new habit because the tension of the game made her want to munch on something and chewing gum was no good as it stuck to her dentures.

She would love to join my circle of wise women if I wanted her to, she said somewhat shyly. But she wasn't sure she had any good advice to give a young girl.

My mother at a loss for advice?! "Of course you do, Mami," I encouraged her. "You've got eighty years of experience! *Más sabe el diablo por viejo que por diablo.*" I quoted the saying she used to quote to us, endorsing her authority. The devil knows more because he's old than because he's the devil. "And besides, you've raised four daughters."

"Okay," she agreed, taking a bite of a saltine. Now it wasn't the game but my question making her nervous. "I guess I'd tell her she better be prepared. You have to be able to take care of yourself. You don't know if you're going to be divorced someday and have to raise kids on your own. Don't depend on anyone but yourself!"

Again, as with my other wise women, the woman warrior was being summoned.

"Another thing is that if there's something you love to do, do it. Like if you want to spend ten hours in a room writing, do it, and don't let anyone tell you you should be giving it up or keeping your husband company. It's the quality time that counts."

Cheers and the excited voice of the announcer. Big Papi was up to bat, Mami informed me, nervously biting into another cracker.

I, too, was feeling the need to chew on something so as not to blurt out, "Mami!!!" You see, during my last visit, she had cautioned me that I had better get ready to let go of my writing. "You're going to get old, you know. You can't keep doing that writing day in and day out."

Although we hardly ruffled each other's feathers anymore, this comment had ruffled mine. "Well, I am not going to give it up, Mami," I informed her. "Writing is how I live my life." She had shaken her head as if she knew better. "It's a calling, Mami, not a job. The best thing I could wish somebody is to find their calling, not let anyone make them give it up!"

Somehow my impassioned defense of my writing months ago had dissolved her absolute certainty of what was right for me. In fact, the wisdom my wise-woman mami was now handing down she had gotten a few months earlier from me!

But because of talking to Mami, I do get wiser. How could I think I could round up a bunch of women and harvest wisdom from them for everyone's use? Wisdom is not a fixed quality. It circulates among us. No wonder I found it so hard trying to decide whom to include in my circle of wise women. Wisdom happens in relationship, in a context of the back-and-forth. Aniana Vargas, a very wise Dominican woman who stayed on working with *campesinos* after her companion revolutionaries went down the mountain to their plush jobs and comfortable lives, once told me that everything that is known in the world is known among all of us. *Todo lo que se sabe en el mundo se sabe entre todos.* Our joint wisdom is the great river into which our little rivulet lives and books flow, and it is that river that we can help our young people learn about and access and navigate on their very own.

Mary Pipher, whom I contacted right before my call to Mami, had begun to steer me toward this realization. She had graciously agreed to be interviewed but declined to offer a *consejo*. "Sage advice all starts sounding the same," she explained. "Be true. Follow your North Star. Listen to your inner voice. I'd much rather approach my reader as a fellow learner than as a teacher. But here's a thought about your book," she added, as if wanting to give me something. "Think of it as a canoe, and steer us back into the Big Water, into a richer experience of this tradition, with what you have to say."

I had to laugh (my mother's laugh) because here I was getting the most personal and touching *consejo* from the wise woman who had declined offering advice.

And so, I decide to disband my circle of wise women. Because, wise reader, as you've probably realized: it has been my very own *quinceañera* at fifty-six that I've been setting up here at the close of my book! Inviting my favorite women to be part of my court. Asking for their wisdom and their stories, their bendición to cherish and preserve and now pass on.

A Conversation with Francisca "Panchita" Dávila

On the banks of the Mohawk River is the town of Amsterdam, home to one of the oldest and largest Latino communities in upstate New York. Francisca "Panchita" Dávila was one of the people who made the trip to Amsterdam in 1960 from her rural home in Salina, Puerto Rico. Her parents were farmers who grew sweet potatoes, yucca, yams, corn, beans, coffee, and breadfruit. She learned the arts of crochet and tailoring from her mother, Mercedes Torres. They worked together at home, embroidering and sewing for the family but also for other people in the village.

Today Panchita Dávila is a dressmaker and planner of the traditional *quinceañera*. In most urban areas, dresses for the event are bought at stores, but Dávila's dresses are custom made, reflecting the traditions inherent in Puerto Rican society; they are meant to be handed down to the next generation. Dávila's own experiences prepared her for her current role as community seamstress and *quinceañera* planner.

Dávila: I was kind of born with the idea of being a sewer, or better, a designer, but I did not have the opportunity to be a designer. I used to see my mom sewing. That's how little by little I learned how to sew. When I was going to turn fifteen, I did not have any plans to celebrate my fifteenth birthday because we were poor and we were a big family, but all my friends from school came into agreement that I should celebrate my sweet fifteen. They collected five or six dollars, which in that time was a lot of money. With that money I was able to go to a warehouse where they sold materials and that's how I did the first sweet fifteen dress. Then people started asking me to design dresses to go to parties, but my favorite was making dresses for the sweet fifteen.

"A Conversation with Panchita Dávila," first published in *Voices: The Journal of New York Folklore*, vol. 28, Fall–Winter 2002.

The *quinceañera* has two parts—the mass and the fiesta—and both events are filled with symbolic gestures and moments. Like most celebrations, the extent to which the *quinceañera* is celebrated has as much to do with social class and family status as the individual wishes of the birthday girl. But there are some aspects that are common to all *quinceañeras*.

Dávila: For the ceremony in the church, the sweet fifteen girl most of the times comes with seven to eight young couples, symbolizing the number fifteen. Two little kids are chosen to carry the pillows. The boy carries a pillow with the shoes, her first high heels, and the little girl carries a heart-shaped pillow with the crown.

The most symbolic act during the *quinceañera* is the changing of the shoes. The girl's father switches her shoes, from the flats she arrived in, to the high heels she will leave in. Shoes and crowns play a pivotal role in the birthday girl's transformation in the eyes of the community from girl to young woman.

Dávila: At the fiesta, the father dances with his daughter and then the mother takes her and dances with her until they get to the make-believe throne. The crown is put on her head by the mother, and when the girl is sitting, the father comes and takes off her sandals and puts on the high heels. Then the father takes his princess out to dance again and from there the party continues.

Maintaining tradition takes work and Panchita does what she can to make a girl's sweet fifteenth birthday a special one, including working closely with the girl and her family.

Dávila: It costs a lot of money to go to a store and buy a dress for a sweet fifteen; it is like going to buy a wedding dress. When the family come to me, they bring more than one style, and here I help them combine. For example, let's take the bottom part of this dress and the top of the other one. If they are satisfied, I'm satisfied myself.

In the past few years Panchila has noticed some fundamental changes creeping in.

Dávila: When I came to Amsterdam there were many Spanish-speaking people so I made many sweet fifteen dresses. After a while, the daughters didn't want to celebrate the sweet fifteen any longer. They wanted to celebrate the sweet sixteen. But I coordinated the events with a broken heart because I wanted people to keep celebrating the sweet fifteen and to keep the culture alive forever.

To Panchita Dávila the *quinceañera* is more than just a birthday party.

Dávila: The *quinceañera* is important because from that day on the sweet fifteen girl can find a good path to become a better person with new ideas, because until that day everything was made easy for her, everything was beautiful. Now she will grow up to be a matured person with many responsibilities. Little by little, the sweet fifteen celebrations are becoming history for many of our people.

For Panchita it is a personal quest to keep this tradition alive.

Dávila: I'm always trying to talk to the girls when they are fourteen, and if I know them or the parents know me, I tell the parents, "Next year your daughter is going to be fifteen. Are you going to celebrate her sweet fifteen?" Sometimes they may say, "Oh, but she wants the new generation style." I say, "She is pure Hispanic and in our culture it is important when they turn fifteen. We should keep the culture and not let it die." I'm always talking to the parents and tell them, "I'm here. I can help you in all you'll need." So there can always be a few girls that want to celebrate their sweet fifteen. Anyway, I will keep doing what I believe until the day that I die.

Selected Bibliography

Alvarez, Julia. *Once Upon a Quinceañera: Coming of Age in the USA*. New York: Viking, 2007.

Anzaldúa, Gloria. *Borderlands/La Frontera*. Introduction by Sonia Saldívar-Hull. 2nd edition. San Francisco: Aunt Lute Foundation, 1999.

Cantú, Norma E. "*La Quinceañera*: Towards an Ethnographic Analysis of a Life-Cycle Ritual," *Southern Folklore* 1 (1999).

Glatzer, Richard, with Wash Westmoreland, dir. *Quinceañera*. Sonny Pictures Home Entertainment, 2006.

Horowitz, Ruth. *Honor and the American Dream: Culture and Identity in a Chicano Community*. New Brunswick: Rutgers University Press, 1983.

———. *Teen Mothers: Citizens or Dependents?* Chicago: University of Chicago Press, 1995.

Napolitano, Valentina. *Migration, Mujercitas, and Medicine Men: Living in Urban Mexico*. Berkeley: University of California Press, 2002.

Stavans, Ilan. *Q&A: Latino History and Culture*. New York: Collins, 2007.

INDEX

Adoración Nocturna, 80n8
Alegria, Malin, 115
Alessandrini, Raniero, 24
Allende, Isabel, 118, 119
Altercito (family altar), 48, 60–61n10
Anthropology: and the assumption
that space is discontinuous, 25;
cartography of insider and outsider, 8;
and the cultural determinism model,
9; rescue motif in, 24–25
Anzaldúa, Gloria, 9, 25, 26

Banck, G., 79n1
Bañuelas, Arturo, 13, 14, 15, 16, 28n36
Beard, David, 11–12, 16, 16–17
Beauty pageants, 5; Miss America
Pageant (2001), 5
Bell, B., 37
Benefactor/beneficiary metaphor, 48
Blair, James, 60
Boas, Franz, 24
"Brideland" (Wolf), 115–16
Broccatto, Roberto, 56
Brummel, Mark J., 50–51

Cain, Will, 118
Cantú, Norma E., 49, 49–50, 50, 51, 54, 87,
93, 95, 96, 98, 118, 119–20
Caplow, T., 40
Cardenas Gonzalez, H., 70–71
Carlota (empress of Mexico), 3, 49
Casa chica, 81n14
Castro, Heidy, 86, 88, 88–89, 90–91, 92,
94–95, 98, 100, 104, 105
Casuso, Jorge, 13
Catechism of the Catholic Church, 48

Catholic Church, the: the Archdiocese
of Chicago, and the Mexican population, 11, 24, 27n14, 27nn22–23; the
Archdioceses of Los Angeles and San
Antonio, and regulation of the *quinceañera*, 28n27; *quinceañera* preparation
programs of, 15, 56, 58, 59, 67, 101, 102;
as a "spiritual benefactor" to Mexican
immigrants and their descendants,
47–48; view of the *quinceañera*, 23–24,
25, 50–51, 55–57, 58. See also *Communidades Eclesiales de Base* (CEBs, or Chris-
tian Base Communities); *quinceañera*,
clergy opposition to
Chapple, B. D., 45n2
Cisneros, Sandra, 25, 118, 120
Clifford, James, 8, 24–25
Cohen, Abner, 32
Collier, J., 80n11
Colonia popular, 80n2
Colonialism, 24
Communidades Eclesiales de Base (CEBs,
or Christian Base Communities), 65,
78–79, 79–80n1; attitudes toward
celebrations of "traditional" rituals,
69–71
Compadrazgo, 39–41, 42, 43, 44
Confianza, 40, 45n4
Conway, William, 13, 17
Coon, C., 45n2
Cordi-Marion Sisters, 26n2
Coronado, Caroline, 56–57

Dahm, Charles, 13, 15, 24
Dávila, Francisca "Panchita," 124–26
Davis, F., 32

ABOUT THE EDITOR
AND CONTRIBUTORS

EDITOR

Ilan Stavans is Lewis-Sebring Professor in Latin American and Latino Culture and Five College–Fortieth Anniversary Professor at Amherst College. A native from Mexico, he received his doctorate in Latin American Literature from Columbia University. Stavans' books include *The Hispanic Condition* (HarperCollins, 1995), *On Borrowed Words* (Viking, 2001), *Spanglish* (HarperCollins, 2003), *Dictionary Days* (Graywolf, 2005), *The Disappearance* (TriQuarterly, 2006), *Love and Language* (Yale, 2007), *Resurrecting Hebrew* (Nextbook, 2008), and *Mr. Spic Goes to Washington* (Soft Skull, 2008). He has edited *The Oxford Book of Jewish Stories* (Oxford, 1998), *The Poetry of Pablo Neruda* (Farrar, Straus and Giroux, 2004), *Isaac Bashevis Singer: Collected Stories* (3 vols., Library of America, 2004), *The Schocken Book of Sephardic Literature* (Schocken, 2005), *Cesar Chavez: An Organizer's Tale* (Penguin, 2008), and *Becoming Americans: Four Centuries of Immigrant Writing* (Library of America, 2009). His play *The Disappearance*, performed by the theater troupe Double Edge, premiered at the Skirball Cultural Center in Los Angeles and has been shown around the country. His story *"Morirse está en hebreo"* was made into the award-winning movie *My Mexican Shivah* (2007), produced by John Sayles. Stavans has received numerous awards, among them a Guggenheim Fellowship, the National Jewish Book Award, an Emmy nomination, the Latino Book Award, Chile's Presidential Medal, and the Rubén Darío Distinction. His work has been translated into a dozen languages.

CONTRIBUTORS

Julia Alvarez: Writer-in-Residence, Middlebury College. Author: *How the Garcia Girls Lost Their Accent* (1991), *In the Time of the Butterflies* (1994), *Something to Declare* (1998), *In the Name of Salome* (2000), *Before We Were Free* (2002), *The Woman I Kept to Myself* (2004), *Saving the World* (2006), and *Once Upon a Quinceañera: Coming of Age in the USA* (2007).

Sara Arcaya: Education and Outreach Coordinator, Casa Myrna Vasquez in Boston.

Karen Mary Dávalos: Associate Professor of Chicana/o Studies at Loyola Marymount University. Author: *Exhibiting Mestizaje: Mexican (American) Museums in the Diaspora* (2001). Co-editor: *The Chicano Studies Reader: An Anthology of Aztlán, 1970–2000* (2001).

Francisca "Panchita" Dávila: Seamstress in Amsterdam, a town in upstate New York.

Kristen Deiter: Director of Records Management and Archives at Marywood University. Author: *The Tower of London in English Renaissance Drama* (2008).

Ruth Horowitz: Professor of Sociology at New York University. Author: *Honor and the American Dream: Culture and Identity in a Chicano Community* (1983) and *Teen Mothers—Citizens or Dependents?* (1995).

Karal Ann Marling: Professor of Art History at the University of Minnesota. Author: *Wall-to-Wall America: A Cultural History of Post-Office Murals the Great Depression* (1982), *George Washington Slept Here: Colonial Revivals and American Culture, 1876–1986* (1988), *As Seen on TV: The Visual Culture of Everyday Life in the 1950s* (1994), *Graceland: Going Home with Elvis* (1996), *Illusions of Eden: Visions of the American Heartland* (2000), *Looking North: Royal Canadian Mounted Police Illustrations— The Potlatch Collection* (2003), and *Debutante: Rites and Regalia in American Debdom* (2004).

Valentina Napolitano: Assistant Professor of Anthropology at the University of Toronto. Author: *Migration,* Mujercitas, *and Medicine Men: Living in Urban Mexico* (2002). Co-editor: *Encuentros antropológicos: Power, Identity and Mobility in Mexican Society* (1998).

Judith Ortiz-Cofer: Professor of English, University of Georgia, Athens. Author: *Terms of Survival* (1987), *The Line of the Sun* (1989), *Silent Dancing* (1991), *The Latin Deli* (1993), *The Year of Our Revolution* (1998), *Woman in Front of the Sun* (2000), *The Meaning of Consuelo* (2003), and *A Love Story Beginning in Spanish* (2005).